ANTIQUE HARDWARE

P R I C E   G U I D E

A comprehensive collector's price and identification guide to vintage doorknobs, door bells, mail slots, hinges, door pulls, shutter hardware and locksets

H. WEBER WILSON

Table of Contents

1. Introduction to Antique Hardware

2. American Hardware Artistry

3. American Hardware in American Buildings

4. Figural & Emblematic Hardware

5. Hardware for Doors

6. Clear Glass Doorknobs

Special Color Section

7. 150 Years of Doorknob Designs

8. Miscellaneous Builders' Hardware

9. They Loved the Lions

Chapter 1
Introduction to Antique Hardware

Buying, Selling & Collecting Antique Hardware

At a time when the interest in antiques and collectibles is at an all time high, the category of antique builders' hardware is very much under-appreciated and undervalued. Just a quick survey of the variety, beauty and quality of antique knobs, bells, hinges, sash locks and shutter pulls proves the potential of this vast new field of collecting that is waiting to be discovered, understood and enjoyed.

There is a small but strong market that is active and evolving, but there are also many "Closet" collectors of door hardware who are yet to be

The classic cultures of Greece and Rome have been the sustaining design influence in America. Thus it is no surprise that some of the earliest decorative hardware in this country would feature heroic images such as warrior profiles. Figural knobs such as these from the 1870s are very collectible and sell in the $100-$300 range.

identified. Over many years of buying and selling a wide variety of antiques, I have always asked about doorknobs. Although most people answer that question with a look that says, "Are you nuts?", it's surprising how many times the response has been: "Yes, I have box in the basement that I saved when such and such building was torn down. I just couldn't see those wonderful things going to the dump."

This long lasting appreciation of well-designed and well-cast architectural fittings would certainly be understood by the creators of 19th century industrial artwork. They lived in a time when it was an expected and accepted fact of economic life that even something as utilitarian as a doorknob should be beautiful, as well as functional. The 19th century was an era of unequaled architectural creativity, with hundreds of thousands of buildings constructed that needed quantities of builders' hardware. In addition, there were dozens of disparate architectural styles used. These two factors give today's hardware collectors a treasure trove of wondrous items to search for.

This book presents an initial review of antique builder's hardware and presents the principal collector categories in the context of the architectural era in which they were created. Where possible, I have provided names of manufacturers and dimensions.

Wrought-steel door plate in the form of a medieval knight. Note the keyhole as the mouth of a lion. SC/100-300

Value & Condition

As an important extension of this factual material, I have provided a value guide based upon the market in which I am buying and selling antique hardware today. Every antique has special properties and each buyer and seller has specific reasons that are important to them on a given day. A single price is therefore only valid for a single sale and so the values attached to the hardware shown in this book are presented in two different contexts and each context is given wide parameters. The first issue for determining value is importance. This can mean rarity, condition or what I call "Collectibility." Usually, all three factors should be carefully considered.

The mighty lion was often rendered in hardware designs, but never better than in this entry knob and plate designed by Ludwig Kreuzinger in the late-1860s. SC/2000+

Rarity is the most ethereal of these terms and needs to be factored in with great caution. The world of antiques is filled with stories of precious items bringing huge sums the first time they are sold. News of the strong sale then shakes out numerous other examples, which invariably drives the next sale price considerably lower. This potentiality is especially true for hardware collectors because there are so many things yet to be found. Even more important is the reality that most serious collectors have things that almost no one else has seen—and most of the players still don't know one another.

On the other hand, someone who has built a serious collection of hardware may well recognize a piece to be truly rare and then buy it for practically nothing because only he or she has the attendant knowledge. The next price of that piece will be extravagant, providing the new owner can find a new buyer with at least the same level of appreciation.

Consequently, for those who have followed my phone/fax auctions and will now compare those results with the price ranges I offer here, certain discrepancies will be evident. This is the natural order of things, I believe, for is not the difference between what something brings at auction and how that same item fares in subsequent markets the juice that provides the fun and adrenaline for the our collector personalities?

After rarity, the next question to consider is the practical and quantifiable concept of condition. In this area, as long as we can remember a few key tenants, we can then make excellent collecting decisions. The basic rule is: "Don't buy anything that shows damage." But as every collector knows, this is much easier said than done, because great things with a "Little damage" can be bought at bargain prices. In the hardware sector, this temptation is softened somewhat by the fact most things collectors seek are made of cast metal; therefore, repairs are very difficult or impossible. Nonetheless, the concept of condition goes will beyond nicks, dents and gouges. Many a great doorknob or backplate has had the delicate casting details wiped out by over-polishing. Many other fine fittings have been bent, twisted or otherwise brutalized during removal. Both these conditions result in an item being considerably less interesting and valuable.

An important adjunct to the question of damage is the question of wear. Most hardware was made of metal, and it was being constantly touched and turned, so many great items show up with details that have all

At the high point of popularity for decorative hardware in the 1890s, homeowners could order a dozen or more different items in the same pattern. This diminutive cupboard pull in Reading's popular "Columbian" pattern is only 5" long and 1.25" wide. The keyway is 0.75" long. SC/100-300

Condition is the critical factor for determining quality and this cherub sunburst passage knob is crisp and clean. This cherub face is often found with a flattened nose, which diminishes the value considerably. SC/100-300

Above: This lady knob is not often found, so even though the wear is considerable, it is nonetheless desirable. Note the date of 1878 on the reverse. SC/500+

Russell & Erwin made some fantastic oversize door plates in the mid-1870s. This one, 10.5″ long, features Neo-Grec details of all varieties and a pair of fanciful beasts bracketing the two keyholes. SC/300-500

but disappeared. Therefore, pay a premium for hardware that retains its crisp casting and stay away from that you would consider a lesser grade. As your knowledge expands, you'll learn about certain desirable doorknobs have only been found in very worn condition. Then one day you'll pay strong money for something that's all but ruined, because you believe it's the only one ever seen.

The next concern about condition relates to color and surface. Many hardware collectors want every piece polished to the nines and that's fine if you plan to hold whatever you own. In terms of market value, however, serious collectors pay premiums for old surfaces and "As found condition." Don't ever polish a doorknob you plan to resell. Removing built up grime and even old paint, is usually possible without harming the surface, but practice you techniques on pieces you might have to throw away.

A few words about color are also in order. Old materials, whether metal, wood, or even plastic, develop a surface patina that is as individualistic and desirable as old wine. Hardware collectors are especially fortunate be-

An Aesthetic-style banded-edge passage knob which appears to be a variation on the popular "Broken Leaf" pattern by Lockwood. Note the ferns and the Greek key design. HH/300

cause we are primarily interested in items made from bronze, brass and other metals which will mellow into innumerable shades of red, rose, verdigris and gold. Not a small aspect of these appealing colors is the fact that they are the result of countless contacts with a human hand, stretching over 100 years or more. Therefore, be extremely cautious with any attempts at cleaning or polishing. When in doubt, offer you hardware "As is." Serious buyers know what they are looking at and they will be happy to do whatever "Tuning up" they deem necessary.

Three small hardware pieces: a double-keyhole door plate, a pull-down bell lever and a covered keyhole escutcheon. Each of these has been trimmed to fit the molding of the door on which they were installed. Study value only.

The final consideration for condition is completeness. Learn how hardware was made, what functions it was designed to accomplish and what parts made up the whole piece. For example, an easy exercise would be to study double-keyhole front door plates. Most of them had a swinging cover over the lower key-hole, but many did not. Learn how to be certain if that critical part is missing. Another checkpoint when looking at door plates is to sure they have not been cut down or otherwise trimmed to fit the dimensions of a particular door. This happened more often that you think; after 100 years or more, the evidence is not always easy to spot.

There are plenty of other things to discover, such as missing parts to doorbells, replacement thumb latches on door handles and electric bell buttons being soldered on plates originally designed for T-levers. Remember, people used what was available and made simple repairs that worked. They weren't thinking about doorknob

A Neo-Classical-style thumb-latch door handle, c1930. Although these handles can show beautiful color and patina, they are of almost no interest to collectors or homeowners. SC/15-30

Single door pulls are of less interest than pairs. This is the "Mooresque" pattern by Corbin, c1895, and shows beautiful shades of red and gold, 18.5" x 3.25".

HH/50-150

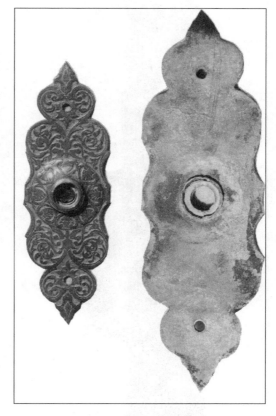

Plate for a doorbell pull, c1875, that was later modified to accept an electric bell button. Always look at the back side of hardware for the mark of the maker-or evidence of a klutzy handyman. Study value only.

Experienced collectors will know that this doorbell pull is not the same pattern as the doorbell plate. HH/30-100

A store door handle in the popular "Broken Leaf" pattern by Lockwood. SC/100-300

collectors who might be coming 100 years down the road.

When we prepare the catalogs for our phone/fax auctions, we try very hard to offer only those items which have "No apologies." At the same time, we are careful to point out anything that might be of concern to a serious collector. In this book, however, I have refrained from specific comments on condition, as I consider the pictures as illustrative only and presume the values assigned to be for examples without significant flaws.

All this discussion then, leads to the third issue in determining the importance of a particular item. I call this issue "Collectibility," by which I mean "Relative market demand." For example, it is sometimes worthwhile buying an outstanding example of a common item and it is sometimes good strategy to buy a hard-to-find item in poor condition. These are individual decisions that are honed only from being part of many buy-sell situations. The "Collectibility" values I have assigned to the hardware in this book reflect my personal experiences and preferences and are open to comments from interested collectors.

Collecting Categories Used in this Book

Creating categories is a challenge and I expect that what I present here will at some point be modified. My goal at this time is to have fewer rather than more parameters and to begin building a consensus on levels of importance. Every collector has his or her own sense of which pieces are more or less important—serious collectors know that these judgments are constantly changing. So here are my collectibility criterion and a brief explanation of how I have applied them to this book.

SC—Serious Collector Quality
HH—Hard to Find and Highly Desirable
XQ—Exceptional Quality in Design, Materials and/or Finish
FF—Frequently Found But Fine Examples are Always in Demand
BC—Beginning Collector Quality

SC—Serious Collector Quality

Items that are rarely if ever seen, or have broad agreement among experienced collectors of a sustaining importance. Usually these items will command a premium price.

An entry knob with the American eagle from the original Department of State in Washington, D.C. Beautiful work both front and back. SC/1000+

(SC—Serious Collector Quality...continued)

Mallory Wheeler produced some of the best decorative hardware in the late-19th century. This passage knob with grape motif retains its original gilding. SC/500+

A small gilded oval doorknob with a Chinese man. SC/500+

The Seated Stag knob by Corbin, c1870s, was originally installed in the Connecticut state capital in Hartford. SC/1000+

HH—Hard to Find and Highly Desirable

Items that may be found in many collections, but are infrequently offered in the market. These items have a broad consensus of superior quality and are displayed with pride and appreciation. Generally the price expectation for these items is strong.

This "Bear claw" entry knob is the "Ercola" pattern by Yale, c1890. HH/500+

Knobs with unusual shapes, such as this shell form passage knob, are always desirable. HH/100-300

(HH—Hard to Find and Highly Desirable...continued)

*Another oversize door plate by R&E.
Note the rat bodies with eagle heads and
the lion face around the keyhole. Coinage
quality casting, 1870s, 10" long.*

HH/300-500

XQ—Exceptional Quality in Design, Materials and/or Finish

Items with a self-evident quality of workmanship and materials. These pieces may not be the top of a manufacturer's line, but they nonetheless represent the very best of hardware artistry. Given the inherent quality of these items, they are usually quite affordable and excellent additions to intermediate and advanced collections.

Gilded passage knob by Branford with Neo-Grec and Aesthetic details.
XQ/100-300

Gilded keyway for a cylinder lock, cast with a lion face. XQ/100-300

The "Muffin" knob has an appealing form and a rich brown patina. XQ/50-150

(XQ—Exceptional Quality in Design, Materials and/or Finish...continued)

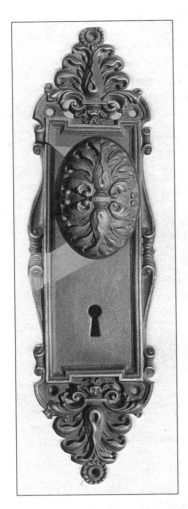

Aesthetic passage knob with bulbous back plate by Nashua. Note lotus flower, fern designs and the little screw heads cast into top of the knob.

XQ/100-300

Crisp entry knob and plate in the "Pavia" pattern by Corbin is a good example of the Neo-Classical style.

XQ/100-300

Keyhole escutcheons can be found in many interesting shapes and sizes Many have two keyways and a swinging keyhole cover. XQ/30-100 each

FF—Frequently Found
But Fine Examples are Always in Demand

Items that were produced in large quantity and show up regularly in the market. Certain patterns are very collectible. Watch for the low-production items, such as bell plates, door slots and sash locks and then buy the outstanding pieces when the price is right. In general, the Northeast States have more hardware than elsewhere because this is where it all began. So what we think of as Frequently Found, such as tapered shank glass knobs, may be scarce in other locales.

Three frequently found doorknob patterns that are always appreciated by collectors and homeowners. FF/15-30 each

(FF—Frequently Found But Fine Examples are Always in Demand...continued)

Doorbells are a separate area of collecting and many highly decorated examples can be found. This one is cast iron, nicely decorated and marked with the maker's name and patent date on back. FF/50-150

A large door plate from an Elks buildings. Lots of hardware with fraternal decoration is found, so buy what is unusual and is in very good condition. FF/50-150

Mortise locks are generally of minor interest to hardware collectors. Don't pay much unless the front plate is decorated, or is something you need to complete a set. FF/30-100

BC-Beginning Collector Quality

Common items that have some redeeming value such as an especially interesting design or a great color. Much hardware of the early 20th century falls into this category, due primarily to the lower quality materials that were used. These items can be excellent knowledge builders, but buy only perfect examples at minimum prices.

Knobs that have a tubular shank/spindle combination are not popular because they are hard to display. Buy them only if they are special. BC/15-30

Thin, stamped hardware is low quality, thus has low value. Pocket door hardware is not especially popular. Lightweight knobs are a good indication of light interest. BC/15-30

There are many painted porcelain knobs around. Before you buy, learn to distinguish hand painting from transfer prints. This low-quality knob dates from c1900. BC/15-30

(BC-Beginning Collector Quality...continued)

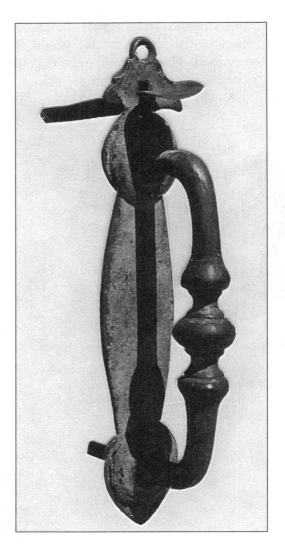

Even though iron or brass door latches like this date from the 1820s or earlier, they don't generate much interest among today's collectors. BC/15-30

Cast iron hardware always brings considerably less than examples cast in bronze. Lots of interesting miscellaneous items, such as these bale handles, can be found very reasonably. SC/15-30

Price Ranges Used in this Book

My basic philosophy when buying something, be it a new house or a doorknob, is that the least import information is the asking price. First, the item must be right and then there must be good reasons to consider the purchase. After that comes a decision as how much I want to pay and then consider what value the seller has established. Sometimes this process takes a week; sometimes it takes 30 seconds. In the end, I hope that my value and the seller's value are close. Then we can negotiate a happy price for both parties.

When buying at auctions, this process is different, because the distinct time element and competitive egos can upset otherwise rational decisions. As an auction seller, however, I have the advantage of watching prices develop (or not) and see just how close my predictions are. Over the past three years, we have auctioned nearly 1,000 antique hardware lots, many of which contained multiple items. Over 80% of this material sold for at least the opening bid and most of the better quality items have brought prices close to or exceeding our expectations.

Therefore, the price ranges attached to each illustration in this book are based on knowledgeable appraisals and real prices-realized. There are eight different ranges which conform roughly to the price points we see in our hardware sales, but I've also allowed plenty of room for a willing buyer and willing seller to haggle. Readers will also note that just because an item is given a strong rating on the collectibility scale, that alone does not dictate a particular price range.

Obvious situations aside, this leaves plenty of room for the most important factor to come into play: knowledge. So the last lesson is the same as the first: learn as much as you can and you will build a collection that will bring you great satisfaction. And that is priceless.

This curved-edge, beaded-border octagon passage knob has a Druid face and wreath. It looks as if it would bring a good price, but it is nickel-plated, which is usually a depreciating factor. SC/100-300

Some of the early decorative doorknobs of the 19'860s and 1870s were cast in lead and then covered with a thin copper foil. This entry knob with a classic female profile also has an unusual scalloped backplate. Even though this piece shows typical roughness where the foil has worn away, it is an important example of early decorative work. SC/500+

A Wonderful Sad Story

Everyone looking at the accompanying photos already knows the end of this tale and every doorknob collectors can probably feel both the elation and the heartache I felt when this doorknob was brought out in response to my question of, "Do you have anything with people or animals?" And, in case any new collectors are wondering, no, there was no hesitation about buying this one—even before I knew what the price was going to be.

I knew by the form of the knob that this was early and somewhere a bell rang that suggested that this was pretty important, as well. So what's a machine screw through the face of the stag? Just an apology to a perfectionist, I figured.

Once back home, I stashed this knob in my rat hole for "Historical keepers" and every now and then would take it out and have a little cry. Then one day I looked again at the photo of an old poster that showed the original MCCC/R&E designs and there it was—right in the top row. Then I checked the notes, and, by golly, it said that there are no known examples of this Standing Elk knob.

Well lookee here! This is as close as I've come to a true one-of-a-kind item, but even I have to admit that the condition could be better. So what's the value? Probably pretty high if I sell it before this book comes out. After that, we may see several of these fall out of the woodwork and then the good old free-market will give us the answer. SC/2000+

Top view of the Standing Elk, as found. The modern screw has been removed, as has all the detail of the face!

This knob was cast in two pieces, with the top screwed on from the inside, not the outside.

The Part is as Good as the Whole

Antiques markets are the best places to find good hardware and this oval buffalo was laying in a showcase just waiting for me I guess. The owner knew it was a doorknob and that it was unusual and didn't hesitate to ask a strong price. I didn't hesitate to buy it.

With or without a shank, this knob represents the very best of American hardware artistry and to date I know of no other examples. For me, the part is as good as the whole and I even like the casting tab. It gives sets the perfect tone for a wonderful work in progress.

Someday I expect to see the complete knob and hope I can afford to buy it.

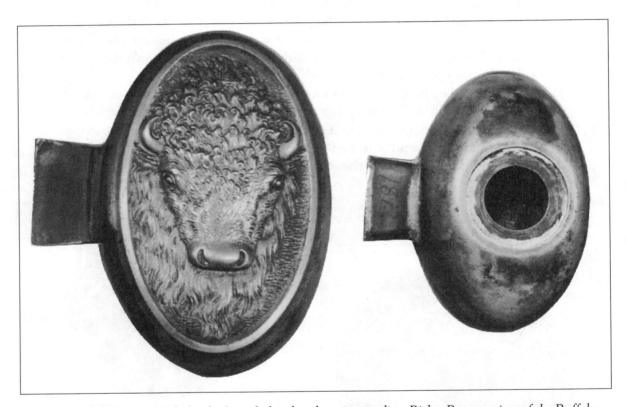

Left: Top view of the Buffalo knob. Superb detail and casting quality. Right: Reverse view of the Buffalo knob showing where the shank would be attached. The mold tab on the side would be removed and polished off during the finishing process. SC/1000+

A Well Turned Doorknob

Brief History of Decorative Hardware in America

Moving from room to room, or out to the garden and back, is one of life's constant, yet ever changing rhythms. We take for granted the threshold that marks both "In" and "Out" and rarely recognize that the swinging door is only as good as the hinges on which it pivots, the lock that keeps it open or closed and the simple doorknob that makes everything work without a hitch. (See large drawings of these building styles starting on page 45.)

Pilgrim century doors were opened with wrought iron thumb latches. In the 18th century, surface-mounted mechanical locks were widely used, with a simple brass ball that could be grasped and turned. Occasionally, these early knobs were made from sterling silver or were silver-plated. The vast majority of builder's hardware, however, remained finely crafted, but non-ornamental.

By the early 1830s, America was booming, thanks to abundant resources and waves of immigrants who used their new political and social freedom to reach for their dreams. Primary among these aspirations was the desire of most families to own their own home; this lead to the building boom that even continues today.

This sarcophagus-shaped door plate and sunken center doorknob was designed and produced by Hopkins & Dickenson in the late-1870s. The originality of form and the beautiful adaptation of both Neo-Grec and Aesthetic motifs underscores the quality and creativity of American industrial art in the third quarter of the 19th century.

SC/300-500

The blockade of American ports during the War of 1812, which caused a severe lack of imports, turned out to be just what the United States needed to jump-start its fledgling economy. For too long, the country had been dependent upon foreign and (especially) British goods. So American entrepreneurs went to work to make the country self-sufficient. The result was that within two decades, the United States had vaulted to the top echelon of world powers and was poised to begin perhaps the greatest economic expansion of all time.

We look around today, craning our necks to see the tops of buildings and forget that only 160 years ago, there was barely a building in the country that rose more than a few stories, or was not was built on a predicable footprint. In the space of just a few years, the entire man-made landscape exploded into a melange of turrets, towers, sprawling floor plans and vast institutional buildings. Within this revolution of architectural design and consumer expectations, there developed a wide spectrum of special product industries: carved stone, sawn wood, cast iron, stained glass and highly ornamental builders' hardware.

Early American

Also by the 1830s, the Greek Revival style had become America's "National style" and temple-fronted, white-painted buildings, both large and small, sprang up from the Atlantic to the Mississippi. In many ways, this rather benign-built environment helped unite our young nation, which was poised on the brink a tremendous social and economic surge that would continue right into the 20th century.

Greek Revival

Even though most Greek Revival buildings were built before the advent of decorative hardware, Classical design was still the dominating influence for American artists. Thus is not surprising that a Greek or Roman warrior profile would appear on some of the earliest figural doorknobs. Note the addition here of the Greek key border. SC/100-300

The door hardware used in these 19th century classical buildings continued to depend upon surface-mounted, wrought iron locks which were primarily activated by iron thumb latches, levers or simple brass knobs. Some of the finer homes undoubtedly had hardware that was silver- or gold-plated and knobs of exotic wood or even ivory were also occasionally used, but examples are very hard to find.

Early American homes used surface mounted locks that were often operated by relatively small brass doorknobs. These examples show both round and oval forms and also show the size of the handmade shanks. BC/15-30

The first mortise locks appeared around the mid-19th century and were often relatively thin and deep. This one retains the original mercury glass doorknobs and disc rosettes. Note the straight "Barrel" shanks. FF/50-150

Along with the brass doorknobs, many early doors were opened with wrought iron thumb latches like these. Early 19th century hardware has not yet found an appreciative public, which is good news for bargain hunting collectors. BC/15-30

Due the huge expansion of the American glass industry in the second quarter of the 19th century, however, many high quality East Coast homes were fitted large cut glass or pressed glass doorknobs. These early glass knobs were hollow, with a hole drilled through the top, so that a hand-wrought spindle could be inserted into the knob and then secured with a handmade brass screw. A number of these early glass knobs have been identified, but there is a vast of amount early-19th century hardware history yet to be discovered and discussed. Be careful not to confuse dresser and furniture pulls with doorknobs.

Sandwich-style pressed and cut glass doorknobs are neither well documented nor understood. They date from the second quarter of the 19th century and represent the efforts of early American glass companies to expand the market for their suddenly affordable products. These three knobs are all the same pattern: one is an entry knob, one is a passage knob and one is a pull for a dresser drawer. (See Chapter 3 for values.)

Suffice it to say that while these austere, symmetrically classical buildings served as the architectural foundation of the nation, they simultaneously generated a pent-up urge to try something new. And thus, when alternative, Romantic building styles suddenly emerged, America gleefully embarked on a 60-year journey into unlimited forms, style and decorative details.

As noted by architectural historian Alan Gowens: *"...by the 1840s, the whole rational of the (Classical) revivals had collapsed...originally conceived as a symbol of political liberty, they had been extended in so many diverse and contradictory ways as to become virtually meaningless...Freedom of business from government...freedom of government to regulate...freedom of religion and freedom from religion...freedom from slaves and freedom to keep slaves...the rights of free labor and the privileges of free capital...the wonder is...that the Greek & Roman revivals dominated American architecture as long as they did."*

The first of the brand new building styles emerged in the 1840s and is known as the Gothic Revival. These castellated, rusticated, gingerbreaded buildings set a decorative benchmark for the following decades and Gothic exuberance was extended to cottages, manor houses and even steamboats.

At about the same time, the Italianate villa-style was introduced and these light, airy and pastoral homes gained im-

Gothic

The original 1840s Gothic Revival in America was primarily residential did not include decorative hardware. Later, around the turn of the century, the Gothic style emerged again in church architecture; this time, the hardware manufacturers produced an enormous quantity of very fine fittings for doors, windows and built-in fixtures. This late-19th century Gothic hardware takes direct inspiration from medieval designs. It was often cast from iron, as well as bronze, and was generally of very high quality. Cast iron door pull (FF/50-150); bronze knob and rosette in the "Hatton" pattern by Yale & Towne (XQ/100-300)

Italianate

mediate popularity, especially in the environs around the cities and commercial centers. Italianate homes featured large windows and fancy brackets under the eaves and the better interiors were fitted with a sleek combination of white marble and black walnut.

Significantly, in these ante-bellum decades, the construction industry was virtually re-invented as well. The "Balloon frame," so called because it went up like a balloon when compared to the old post and beam process, meant that homes could be built in a relative flash. Aiding this new technique was the introduction of machine-made nails and standardized lumber. This was soon followed by the adaptation of central heating, after which anyone could have a home as spacious and sprawling as funds allowed.

By mid-century, trained (or self-proclaimed) architects discovered that Residential Pattern Books could be economically published and then efficiently distributed by the new U.S. Mail service. All who was dreaming of owning their own home could now study an unlimited variety of elevations and floor plans and read detailed information about everything from "Plumber's blunders" to "Speaking tubes." Every building ornament from sawn wood ornament to decorative terra cotta was illustrated in fine detail, but decorative builder's hardware was not.

Fortunately, the hardware companies began to publish their own catalogs, so we have a pretty good record of how decorative doorknobs evolved. Until the late-1860s, hardware companies primarily offered black and white porcelain and fired clay or mineral knobs. Beginning in the 1840s, a steadily widening variety of pressed and fancy glass knobs were available and several examples of decorated porcelain knobs have been found. Exotic materials were also used, including ivory, hardwoods and gutta purcha.

A.J. Downing was one of the earliest and most famous Pattern Book authors and he built a large and loyal audience with titles such as *The Architecture of Country Houses Including Designs for Cottages,*

Fancy, cast bronze hardware was not yet available to mid-century American homeowners, but they were nonetheless interested in the latest innovations and decoration. Gutta purcha was discovered and molded into many objects including doorknobs. XQ/30-100

Farm Houses and the Best Modes of Warming and Ventilating. His vision was truly ahead of him time; in 1850, he accurately predicted the appeal of the-soon-to-be-discovered eclectic style of architecture by Americans:

"Elizabethan or Renaissance Style (eclecticism)...in a philosophical point of view...often violates all rules of art and indulges in all manner of caprice. Mere architects and pedantic judges have accordingly condemned it in all ages. Viewed, however, as a style addressed to the feelings and capable of wonderfully varied expressions, from the most grotesque and whimsical to the boldly picturesque and curiously beautiful, we see much in the style to admire, especially for domestic architecture."

This was about all that America needed to hear, for by the end of the Civil War, the importance of duplicating Europe had diminished and Americans were creating our own building styles and all the accouterments to go with them. A new country was opening up, all over again, only bigger and better than anyone had imagined. Mechanical, commercial and political power was abundant; for everyone who worked hard, a good life was eminently possible. Americans wanted to build and they were neither fearful of the future, nor weighted down by the past.

Of course, imported ideas were always helpful (even inevitable), given the influx and influence of all the new immigrants. The best example of this is the emergence of the Mansard roof, which was a 17th century French idea that was adopted as the highlight of America's Second Empire style. These homes bespoke of a real grandeur, both inside and out, and many a great Mansard mansion still exists from the 1860s and 1870s.

A.G. Newman was a company that came and went in the dynamic decades of the 1870s and 1880s. The firm created some fabulous hardware, including this entrance and door plate. Note the exceptionally fine design and detail. SC/1000+

Second Empire

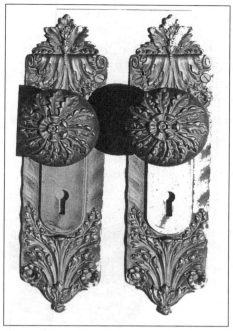

Pair of Neo-Classical passage knobs and plates (9.25" x 2.5" each) in the "Veroccio" pattern by RHCo., gold-washed surface. FF/30-100

It was in these strong, masculine homes that the first seriously decorative bronze hardware was found. The key date is 1869, for that is when the Metallic Compression Casting Company (MCCC) of Boston was awarded its first design patents. Early 1870 saw MCCC bring a folio full of fabulous doorknobs into the market; well before 1875, there was serious competition from half-dozen other companies. Some companies, such as Russell & Erwin (who quickly took over MCCC), continued on into the 20th century, while other companies such as A.G. Newman appeared only briefly but, nonetheless, brightly. In fact, in the rich and prolific history of American hardware artistry, these earliest years were actually the high-water mark of original design, superior materials and exquisite casting.

Of course, Gothic, Italianate and Greek Revival buildings still filled the landscape, and to some American it must have seemed like there was a "Builders Olympics" going on. To fill out the roster, an American entry known as the Stick style also emerged. These homes were invariably built of wood and along with porches, dormers and asymmetrical fenestration, there was an exterior application of boards to emulate the basic framing structure. The concept sounds a little strange, but the results were actually very subtle, creative and honest.

Stick style

Stick-style homes could incorporate the fancy new cast bronze hardware as well as Second Empire, but it is important to note that the primary design influence of these beautiful bronze fittings was powerfully influenced by still lingering Greek Revival style. In fact, this early hardware is best described as Neo-Grec and a close study of the individual design elements shows a plethora of palmettes, Greek keys, anthemions and acanthus. These and other motifs were worked into unendingly delightful designs that matched up well with Americans sense of free expression.

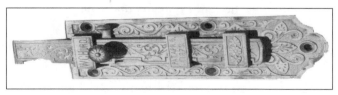

By 1875, the date on this ornate slide bolt, bronze hardware in the Neo-Grec taste had become expected and accepted in every American home of consequence. SC/100-300

The American Stick style, then, fitted out with Neo-Grec hardware, set the stage for the next significant decorative events: the emergence of eclectic or Queen Anne buildings and the Aesthetic or Anglo-Japanese style of interior design. Both of these building styles were introduced to Americans at the Philadelphia Centennial of 1876. Our country was 100 years old and had progressed farther and faster than any other in history. Nonetheless, most Americans had little international exposure, so when the world came to our shores, we were eager to see what was new and then adapt it to our own national personality.

The British exhibit was headquartered in St. George's House, whose gables and half timbers were not a complete surprise, but nonetheless served as the inspiration for what is often called American Queen Anne. These homes are not to be confused with any single historical era, however, and, from the outset, American Queen Anne or free classic homes have brought tears to the eyes of architectural purists. Irregular shapes were piled together with skillful abandon, which then allowed for decorative detail of any quantity and any style. This, of course, was just what Americans wanted; for the next 40 years, hardware companies were delighted fill a massive demand for quantity, variety and originality.

Queen Anne

The Japanese influence, however, was more surprising and much more specific. America had been introduced to the Anglo-Japanese or Aesthetic Movement in the early 1870s by Charles Eastlake and Bruce J. Talbot. Both of these men emphasized simplicity in design; Eastlake, especially, much to his chagrin, had became a household word in a country he never visited. In fact, he finally exclaimed:

"...I feel greatly flattered by the popularity which my books have attained in America, but I regret that their author's name should be associated there with a phase of taste in architecture and industrial arts with which I can have no real sympathy and which by all accounts seems to be extravagant and bizarre..."

By the Centennial, the U.S. was ready to see the real thing and the Japanese pavilion was perhaps the most popular of all the exhibits at the Exposition.

Aesthetic-style store door handle. These flower forms and border designs are repeated on all manner of builders' hardware from the 1880s. XQ/100-300

The Geisha Girl doorknobs by R&E, c1880. Note the varying scale of the entrance, passage and doorbell knobs and how each girl is designed with a different hairstyle. Entry size, SC/1000+, passage size, SC/500+, doorbell pull knob SC/500+

The result was a national demand for what is now called the Aesthetic style, which is the American/European interpretation of primarily Japanese decoration, but which often extends to other Far Eastern and even Middle Eastern cultures.

American hardware manufacturers found that Japanese decorative details were ideal for casting in bronze and American homeowners soon found entire catalogs filled with Aesthetic doorknobs, hinges, sash lifts and banister brackets. The natural forms, such as bamboo and sunflowers, were easy to render, yet powerfully graphic. The birds and butterflies were delightful and the Geisha Girl doorknob by R&E is considered one of the great industrial designs.

The Aesthetic style retained its popularity for more than a decade, but the American Experience was like the crest of a wave; our tastes were constantly turning. Also, because England, France, Italy, Germany and other European cultures were our true antecedents, it wasn't surprising that our tastes were aligned with ideas and forms more closely related to our own ancestors. Thus there emerged alongside the somewhat predictable Aesthetic style, a flamboyant, curvaceous, alternative which in this country has carried the misnomer Victorian, when it

The sunflower was one of the most popular Aesthetic motifs and was the principal design element of many different doorknobs. XQ/50-150

should be really be recognized as an amalgam of Renaissance Revivals, which in and of themselves represent the good old Roman/Greek classical ideals.

Festoons, shells, fans, volutes and classical urns filled with flowers are but a few of the design elements revived by the Renaissance style. American hardware companies tried them all and even spent considerable effort to try and educate their customers on the differences between "Flemish," "Jacobean" and "Louis XIV." In the end, it didn't matter much. American designers mixed and matched motifs and American homebuilders bought what they liked.

American hardware artists of the 1870s had no qualms about using innovating forms to go with their original decorations. Many companies made hexagonal knobs and fancy triangular backplates, but this one by MCCC/R&E was perhaps the first. Note the patent date on the top edge of the ferrule. SC/300-500

The good news for the American economy then and for hardware collectors today, is that the peace, pace and the prosperity of the last quarter of the 19th century saw our country's built-environment expand and express itself without cost concerns or creative inhibitions. One of the great Pattern Book publishers, Palliser & Palliser, said it best in 1878, with this unabashed pitch for the eclectic building style:

"Symmetry applied to private architecture is an invention that has had its day and is completely run out, except in rare cases, where old fogyism holds the sway and rules supreme."

Then Palliser describes one of the new, Stick Style homes in his book as:

"...painted Venetian red, trimmed with Indian red, the chamfers, cut and sunk work being picked out in black...the cost is $1460 and we doubt if there is anyone who can show a prettier home...for the same price. Blessed are they that have homes! Let every man strive to own a home."

A nice Aesthetic passage knob with musical notes and a sunburst. XQ/50-150

This hardware from an entrance set is a good example of how Renaissance revival designs used more motion and detail than the earlier Neo-Grec. How many dolphins can you find?

SC/100-300

In the same year, another great Pattern Book personality, Henry Hudson Holly, expanded on this precept by commenting that:

"...we cannot be said to have any styles and systems peculiarly our own...Yet out of our necessities there have grown certain idiosyncrasies of building which point towards an American style...(in which) we must not hesitate to eliminate those portions for which we have no use or to make such additions as our circumstances demand..."

Americans didn't have to be asked twice. By the mid-1880s, the U.S. stretched from the Atlantic to the Pacific, connected by a transcontinental railroad. People, ideas and materials were moving with unprecedented speed and freedom. Homes, offices, institutions (even fraternal groups) created individualized architecture. Suppliers of decorative building materials, including hardware manufacturers, ramped up their variety and supply.

On the flip-side of this gold coin, we can also see the same surge of innovative construction inexorably forcing the building industry to become better organized, more focused on time and material costs and, therefore, more homogenized. It is no surprise that well before 1900, the economic forces of change were in motion and the great era of decorative buildings, fitted out with fabulous, decorative hardware, was coming to a close.

This fact can be quickly observed by taking a fancy door plate from each decade between 1870 and 1910. Look at the detail of the design, and study the quality of the casting. Then compare the weight of the material.

H&D continued to produce excellent quality hardware up to the turn of the century. This reticulated door set has fine details, but also has considerable area where there is not decoration at all. And that subtly telegraphs the economic facts for hardware companies in the 1890s. They had to reconcile increasing production costs with decreasing consumer interest in fancy hardware and the results are self-evident.

XQ/30-100 each, knob or plate

The conclusions are self-evident: massive demand leads to diluted quality and over-indulgent designs create a desire to return to the strength of simplicity. And this is what occurred in America at the turn of the 20th century. At the same time that eclectic, free classical buildings were reaching their zenith, new decorative forces emerged to present the latest fashions of Art Nouveau and Arts & Crafts. And at the same time, there also appeared the beginnings of the "Modern" movement, as well as a powerful urge to return to America's classical roots. It was a fitting stylistic crescendo to the end of a century.

L'Art Nouveau was the name of a Paris art gallery opened by Samuel Bing in 1895, which became the name of an artistic movement. This style is known for its sensuous curves and highly stylized floral motifs and generated great interest in Europe. By 1900, there was a great amount of Art Nouveau objects and architectural elements in the United States, but the legacy of this style is really just a flair across the horizon of a brand new century. Lots of hardware from the late-1890s incorporates hints of Art Nouveau design, but it never came close to the popularity of the Aesthetic movement.

Americans enjoyed Art Nouveau objects but not Art Nouveau buildings. Thus most Art Nouveau hardware designs were combined with other styles, which in this case is a strong Gothic feel. XQ/50-150

At the same time that Art Nouveau was stirring interest among the *avant garde*, a much more subtle and proletarian style called Arts & Crafts was gaining even greater popularity. The Arts and Crafts movement had begun in England in the 1870s, spearheaded by well-known artists and writers such as William Morris and Edward Burne-Jones. It took most of a decade to extend across the Atlantic, but, once established here, it maintained a strong popularity until well into the 20th century.

The Arts & Crafts movement, which was as much a philosophy as an artistic style, sought to combine hand-wrought medieval techniques with 19th century socialism. The idea of filling one's life with honest and beautiful things was very appealing to Americans and in this country the movement evolved into what we now call the Mission style. And just as the name indicates, Mission or Arts & Crafts objects stressed strong but austere styling, with a minimum of decoration. The Arts & Crafts movement also came along just as the American home was beginning to

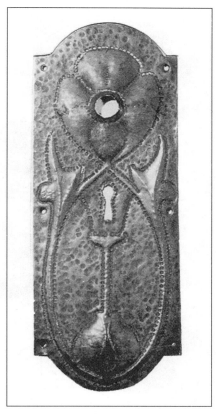

A copper, hand-hammered Art Nouveau/Arts & Crafts door plate. Perhaps a project from one of the many Arts & Crafts workshops that were popular in America in the early-1900s. HH/50-150

dramatically downsize. Economic realities were setting in and a leaner, less fancy style that came to be called "Bungalow" gained the support of both builders and buyers. This fit well into the economic realities of the turn-of-the-century hardware manufacturers, and they were happy to produce extensive lines of lower cost, pseudo-handwrought door

Monel metal is an alloy of nickel and bronze. It was often used in Arts & Crafts hardware, such as this mushroom shaped entry knob and plate. XQ/30-100

By 1910, most residential hardware was becoming more plain rather than more fancy. This entry door set shows how a great look could be produced with minimal design and materials. BC/50-150

and window fittings.

A third new architectural movement emerged at this time as well, lead by Modern architects such as Louis Sullivan and Frank Lloyd Wright. These men sought a brand new dimension for American buildings that would take advantage of modern materials and would emphasizing modern man. It was a long and difficult road, but modern architects moved forward to dominate the much of the 20th century. Hardware from the early buildings of Wright and Sullivan, et. al., is highly collectible, partly because of the name association and partly because of its 1890s quality and style.

As the new century progressed, however, modern buildings became even more plain and basic, except for the occasional homebuilder or designer who cared enough to pay for special orders. All in all, however, the landscape of modern buildings is pretty barren

A doorbell thumb twist with an eagle backplate cut from thin brass. Rather a sad commentary on the state of American decorative hardware by the early-1900s. BC/30-100

By the turn of the century, the "Establishment" had returned to traditional classicism. This doorknob and door plate are from the B&O Railroad. Note how the minimal decoration nonetheless evokes a sense of strength and proven accomplishment. HH/100-300

ground for hardware collectors.

While Art Nouveau, Arts & Crafts and Modern styles were trying to build and maintain a new audience claim market share, the old standby Classicism re-emerged to claim the support and influence it always knew it had. By 1890, there was a stratum of American culture that had built fortunes and social status and wished to create a built environment that returned to symmetry, balance and restraint. This they did, first by creating the temporary buildings of the Great

Classicism

White Way at Chicago in 1893 and then by creating the Mall in Washington D.C. These men of power and position made their statement that ancient orders, after all, were still the best symbols for the world's most progressive country.

This resurgence of Neo-Classic interest was picked up at all levels of building and in all sections of the country. Houses, schools, hospitals and, of course, government buildings returned to unadorned pediments and ionic columns. Hardware manufacturers were right there also, with hundreds of designs that used swags, bellflowers, egg and dart borders and other basic elements taken directly from the Romans and Greeks. Much of this Neo-Classical hardware was very well designed, but, unfortunately, in much of the production, the quality of material was just not as good as back in the 1870s.

This question of quality was affecting all aspects of American building and as competition increased and profit margins shrank, there were failures and realignments throughout the hardware industry. Fortunately, the decades around the turn of the century saw a huge increase in commercial building, and commercial buildings themselves became bigger and bigger. This translated into bigger and bigger hardware orders and because many of these commercial projects opted for custom hardware, there is a vast quantity of very collectible pieces available today. Even government buildings were designed with special doorknobs and hinges, and more than one company concentrated heavily on supplying custom fittings for court-houses,

A modern doorknob and backplate in a design known as "The Rock." This is chrome plate over pseudo-hammered bronze, in an interesting contemporary design. Very good quality, but the mark on the reverse gives us an important clue. It says "Made in Spain." BC/50-150

schools and city halls that were springing up all around the country.

Every door needs a knob (or at least a pull), but expect for the Art Deco movement of the 1930s and 1940s, there hasn't been a decorative style of consequence since World War I. Hardware mechanics have also changed significantly since the 1800s, so a decorative doorknob is just not a viable option to any but the most creative architects today.

Since the 1980s, however, the great resurgence in architectural renovation has brought back an appreciation and rejuvenation of the great hardware of 100 years ago. And now that collectors are adding their interest, knowledge and enthusiasm to this movement, the American legacy of hardware artistry is certain to be appreciated and preserved .

We should never forget the people who came to this country with skill, determination and dreams. It is their unpretentious accomplishments, both artistically and culturally, that provided us with today's collecting pleasures. So when you find one of these Statue of Liberty doorknobs, display it proudly with your best and rarest trophies. XQ/100-300

Various Building Styles With Broad Timelines

Early American or Georgian: 1600s to about 1820

The first 200 years of settlements in North America resulted in little architectural variety. Buildings were primarily rectangular with hipped or gabled roofs and symmetrical fenestration. Structural materials were hand-hewn and builders' hardware was hand-forged. Many homes and public structures had fine decorative details, but, for the most part, the built environment was quite predictable.

Greek Revival: 1820 to about 1860

The Greek Revival style got Americans to move away from the unpleasant memories of Colonial days and took over all aspects of American architecture. It also let houses look like churches and churches look like classical seats of power. The above drawing is of a private home, but it could have also been a school, a government building or a church. The "temple front" was easy to invoke: just turn your building plans so that the end faces the street, then add a couple of columns and a doorway. American liberties with the ancient Greek orders softened the ground and the population for the eccentricities of first the Gothic and later the Free Classic style.

Decorative hardware—primarily glass, porcelain and wooden knobs—began to find its way into such buildings by the 1840s. However, widespread use of decorative hardware would not arrive until the eclectic decades of the 1870s and 1880s.

Gothic: 1840-1860s

The introduction of the Gothic style must have startled most Americans not accustomed to seeing multi-gabled houses with porches, porticos and decorative window treatments. In the 1840s and 1850s, there was little decorative hardware available, so most doors were trimmed with plain porcelain knobs. Gradually these choices expanded to include decorated porcelain, mercury glass and rosewood and carved walnut. Interest in the Gothic style for residential architecture waned by the end of the Civil War.

These "Steamboat Gothic" buildings (the above pair) show how American encrusted and embellished an otherwise staid yet quirky building style into something that was more compatible with a young and restless country. If decorative hardware was available, it would've been used here!

Italianate: 1840s-1860s

The bucolic Italianate Villa was introduced to America about the same time as the Gothic, and its feel of open country was found much more appealing. Note the bigger windows, the wider porches and allure of the rooftop belvedere. Black and white porcelain knobs looked good inside these sleek interiors, but fancy wood and decorative bronze was used where available. Note that whether in an rural or an urban area, the Italianate villa evokes a thought that the owner is a person of substance and property.

American Second Empire
or Renaissance Revival: 1860s-1890s

The introduction of the Second Empire style in the 1860s coincided with the first production of highly decorative bronze hardware. These renaissance-inspired homes, with their mansard roofs and exaggerated fenestration, were an ideal showcase for the artistry of America's fledgling hardware industry. Many of these grand homes were built just before the availability of great hardware, but many more are the source for Kreuzinger Doggies, Kreuzinger Lions and the great figural work of Mallory Wheeler, H&D, A.G. Newman, et. al.

American Stick Style: 1870s-1890s

The Stick Style evolved out of the efforts of American designers and builders to present honest and forthright construction. Thus the wood construction and the overlay of angled clapboards to emphasize the solid and substantial framing underneath. These comfortable, family-oriented homes looked great with any style hardware and provided a broad market for the Neo-Grec styles of the 1870s, as well as innovative Aesthetic designs of the 1880s.

American Free Classic
or Queen Anne: 1880s-1900

Visitors who came to American in the 1880s and 1890s were easily convinced that they were in the land of the free and looking at the homes of the brave. American families wanted big, individualistic homes and American builders complied with homes that bespoke of every era, every culture and every modern consideration.

This Free Classic style made art historians weep, but newly affluent Americans loved the look of Islamic turrets nestled among third story verandahs and overhanging eaves borrowed from a Swiss cottage. Lots of interesting hardware is found on these buildings, but by the mid-1890s much of it began suffering from too much concern for design and not enough concern for quality.

Return to Classicism and Cottages: 1880s-1900s

The move away from intense decoration had begun in the late-1880s, and many people began turning to homes that were inspired by Colonial architecture, the honest labor of the Arts & Crafts movement and the promise of the modern century just ahead. A quick glance at the difference between the roofline of this cottage and the roofline of the Free Classic home will tell you all you need to know about what sort of hardware to expect inside. Plenty of excellent hardware was available up until World War I, but as homes and buildings morphed back into old traditions and a new starkness, there was steadily less demand and therefore less supply.

Pattern Book Ad

Whitney & Rogers is not a known producer of decorative hardware, even though

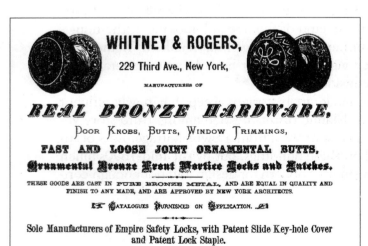

this advertisement from an 1878 pattern book describes them as "Manufacturers." The doorknobs illustrated are designs from P.F. Corbin, so it is probable that the two companies were working with each other. Further research is called for, especially in regards to the "Fast and loose joint ornamental butts."

Profiles and Details of Decorative Doorknobs

Doorknobs come in all shapes and sizes. A close look at the various profiles and some of the decorative details will help you recognize what's special and what's common.

1870s: Pavilion Top, Disc Tops & Sunken Center Knobs

Usually heavy and cast with superbly detailed Neo-Grec designs.

Pavilion top

Disc top

Sunken center

1880s: Drum Form Knobs

Most commonly made in flat or dome tops. Edge area can be incised, recessed or decorated.

Decorated rims

Incised detail

Recessed rim

1890s and Later: Banded Edge Knobs

Usually have a solid, undecorated band around the middle with decorative casting above and below. Hollow, lightweight knobs with undecorated backs are the least desirable; heavy knobs with strong casting details on the reverse are most desirable.

Banded rims

Other Shapes & Details

Many decorative knobs of the 1870s were cast in hexagonal form, then set into triangular backplates. Later, some large fancy knobs were cast in dramatic step-down shapes. Other knobs have knurled edges (a tricky machining process that adds greatly to quality and value). Also look for shanks with a heavy "spread foot."

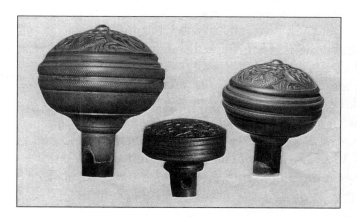 

Knurling

Step-down profile

MCCC/Ludwig Kreuzinger Dog Knob

In the late-1860s, Ludwig Kreuzinger and other designers for the Metallic Compression Casting Company of Boston created the first significant figural hardware in America. This collection of hand-crafted design have rarely been equaled or surpassed. There were numerous designs patented on June 7, 1870, including a lion head, a cavalier or knight profile and a Neo-Grec female profile and several intricate designs, Kreuzinger and MCCC also introduced the "Doggie" knob on that date, and it was immediately acclaimed a masterpiece of industrial art. Today, the doggie knob is considered by many hardware collectors to be their most prized acquisition.

These patents were assigned to Russell & Erwin Hardware, which had the foresight to become sole agents for MCCC, and then quickly buy out the fledgling company. Compression casting created products of exceptional quality; within a few years, R&E moved the foundry operations down to New Britain, CT, and MCCC went out of business.

By the early 1870s, other hardware companies such as Mallory Wheeler and P.F. Corbin had brought out their own lines of solid, beautifully cast bronze hardware, but the original designs of MCCC will always stand as the benchmark of American hardware artistry.

MCCC/R&E doorknobs are often marked on the reverse, and sometimes the patent date is struck on the shank. Likewise, backplates and rosettes are sometimes marked with a patent date on the back or around the shank opening. On doorknobs, one can find three different statements that indicate the evolution of MCCC and its relationship with Russell & Erwin:

"MNF'D BY METALLIC COMPRESSION CASTING CO. BOSTON" *was the original MCCC mark, beginning in the late-1860s. Many of theses knobs also have the patent date of June 7, 1869. stamped on the shank.*

"MFD. BY MET. COMP. CAST. CO. ~~ R.E. MFG. CO. SOLE AGT'S" *was used after the original hardware came on the market and R&E moved to control the new products in the early 1870s.*

"MADE BY RUSSELL AND ERWIN MFG. CO." *was the later mark employed after R&E absorbed MCCC and moved the foundry to New Britain.*

bring a premium, as original MCCC stock is limited. The major concern with this knob is the wear. The Greek palmettes and anthemions around the outside front rim and the serrated rim on the inside often show wear. Also, the nose of the dog is sometimes worn or even flattened. Thus, pay premium prices for premium quality.

SC/2000+

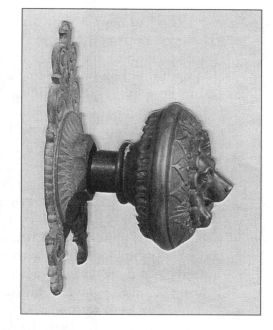

Profile of doggie knob.

The reverse of the doggie knob has one of three different marks.

This triangular rosette is often found behind the doggie knob. It usually but not always has a patent date above the spindle hole.

Angle view of doggie knob.

Reproduction Alert

The bad news is that things made from metal are easy to reproduce. The good news is that most reproduction quality is very poor. Therefore, once you have seen the original of an item, you should not be easily fooled. On the other hand, if you find a rare item and you've never seen the real thing, be wary—especially if you think the price is cheap.

Reproductions are an unfortunate fact in every collectible field and antique hardware is no exception. Happily, however, most people who make repros are into quantity, not quality, so by studying the real and the ersatz, you can learn a lot very quickly. This is especially true with metal castings, because re-casts never have the same crisp detail of the originals. Additionally, recast are always just a little smaller than the originals and often, considerably heavier as well.

Perhaps most important is that most repros look new; the metal is bright and shiny or colored with an unnatural looking patina. Additionally, the makers' marks are smudged or not evident at all and there are often casting blemishes and grinding marks that are very easy to see.

Another key to spotting repros is to be familiar with what items have received the most publicity lately. Repro companies only copy things they think are highly popular, so keep up to date with the hardware market and you'll not likely be surprised.

This lady profile knob looks to good to be true and it is. The casting quality is poor and the weight is excessive. Most important is the fact that there is no screw hole in the shank. The reproducer didn't want to take the time or expense to make doorknob actually useful. Study value only.

This north wind face is a favorite feature in many 19th century decorative compositions, but this doorknob set was cast in the 1980s. The first clue is the quality of the casting, which looks good from a distance but not up close. The second clue is the form and size of the components: they seem small and incompatible. The third (and best) clue is the way the knob is attached to the shank. "Allen" style screws are a modern invention and were never found on old hardware. Likewise, old doorknobs only used a single set screw, never two.

Chapter 2
American Hardware Artistry

Hardware from a Coal Baron's Mansion

In the 1870s, a wealthy man in northeastern Pennsylvania built a mansion fitted with the best bronze hardware from Russell & Irwin. When the house was torn down, someone saved many of the door, window and shutter fittings. Most of these items are found in the R&E catalog of 1873, and many individual pieces are dated 1869 and 1870 in the metal. The figural knobs were not part of the original stash, but might well have been selected by such an affluent homeowner. That all this superb hardware was brought to the mountains of Pennsylvania in the early 1870s tells us a lot about how well the American manufacturing, advertising and distribution system was working.

The plumed knight knob was patented by MCCC/R&E in 1870 and epitomizes the casting artistry of that decade. Passage size. HD/500+

Typical reverse of an MCCC/R&E knob: "Mfd. By Metal. Comp. Cast. Co." and "R.E. Mfg. Co. Sole Agt's." These knobs were also dated at the end of the shank, but this is often worn off.

The lady with bonnet is another original MCCC/R&E design patented in 1870. Watch for excessive wear and faint lettering on reverse. Passage size. HD/300-500

A decorative parlor bell lever with Greek Revival design elements, 3" dia.

EQ/50-150

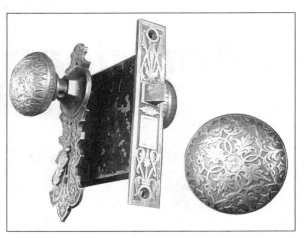

Decorative mortise lock with two MCCC/R&E knobs and Neo-Grec plates that feature Greek palmette keyhole covers and are dated 1870 on the shank. EQ/300-500

Door plate in Neo-Grec style with palmette decorated keyhole cover. XQ/50-150

Finely cast hinges matching the entry lock, 5" x 5". EQ/100-300 pair

A pair of rose bronze
pocket door pulls dat-
ed 1870, 6.75" long.
EQ/50-150

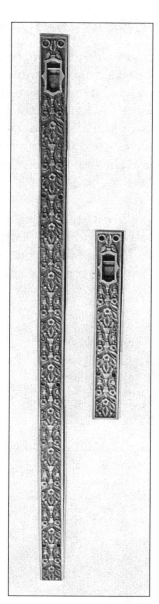

A large and a small flush
bolt matching the R&E
entry door lock, 36" &
12" EQ/100-300

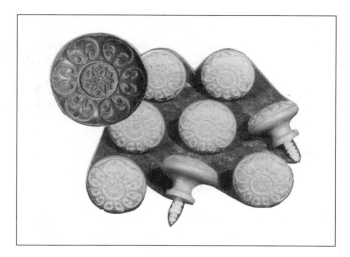

Set of eight bronze shutter pulls in rich
old patina, 1.25" dia.
EQ/100-300 set

Russell & Erwin and its Japanese Collection

R&E, as it is popularly known, began in the 1830s as manufacturers of plate locks and was eventually incorporated as Russell & Erwin in 1846. In 1865, the firm published a 432-page catalog that has become a major resource for hardware collectors, although it pre-dates the great decorative decades of the 1870s and 1880s. In the early 1870s, R&E absorbed the Metallic Compression Casting Company of Boston and began producing what are now considered the pre-eminent examples of American building hardware. In 1902, R&E merged with P.F. Corbin to form the American Hardware Company.

When the popularity of Anglo-Japanese design became the dominant American decorative style in the early 1880s, R&E produced its now famous Japanese collection. These knobs, plates and other pieces make up one of the most desirable groups of hardware for collectors today.

Three different Geisha Girl doorknobs can be found in three sizes, and each lady has a different coiffure. Entry size, SC/1000+, passage size, SC/500+, doorbell pull knob SC/500+

Passage size door plate featuring a geisha girl in her bamboo-covered summerhouse, with bluebirds and clouds overhead. Knob 2.25", plate 5.5" x 5.5". Marked Russell & Irwin and dated 1878. These plates were used behind several different knobs. Passage size plate SC/300-500, entry-size plate, SC/500+

Geisha Girl doorknobs with complementary backplates. This group is highly prized by hardware by collectors.

The double-bluebird doorknob. Marked on reverse and dated 1878 on the shank. Passage size SQ/ 300-500, entry-size SQ/500+

Side view and reverse view of R&E Japanese collection doorknob. Marked "Russell & Erwin Mfg. Co. New Britain Conn. U.S.A." Note the beaded, inset rim and date at end of the shank.

The flying crane doorknob. Passage size SC/300-500, entry-size SC/500+

Single bronze 6" x 6" hinge with Japanese figures and floral scenes. "Pat. Jan 13, 1880." Note the same clouds as seen on the bluebird doorknob. SQ/100-300

Single hinge with Japanese figures and parasol finials. Cast iron with bronze patination.

HH/50-150

Single hinge with cranes. Cast iron with bronze patination. HH/100-300

Aesthetic-style keyhole cover—a little gem, 2" x 1". EX/30-100

P.F. Corbin

Phillip Corbin organized Corbin Hardware in 1849 with a group of relatives and friends from Hartford, CT. The company issued its first catalog in 1852. In 1854, it merged with North & Stanley, an early American lock company. They specialized in locks, but soon moved into decorative hardware and became one of the largest American hardware companies. In the early-1900s, Corbin even began a short-lived automobile enterprise and produced several hundred vehicles. In the 1902, P.F. Corbin and Russell & Erwin were merged into the American Hardware Corporation.

Many of Corbin's large and detailed catalogs have survived, so its comprehensive hardware line can be studied in detail. The firm is also known for its Special Hardware division that specialized in high quality, custom hardware for businesses, institutions, fraternal organizations and government buildings.

Large plate for an octagonal knob, c1874-1875. XQ/50-150

Nickel-plated doorbell pull and escutcheon c1875. HH/100-300

Sunken center knob, patented April 29, 1873. SC/100-300

A striking sunburst passage knob c1875. Beautiful design on reverse. FF/30-100

Bronze French door handle in the same form and pattern Corbin used for its enameled pieces, 4" x 2". XQ/50-150

A fine passage knob and plate (10" x 3") from an Elk's Lodge. Corbin Special Hardware, c1900.

XQ/100-300

Small bronze covered keyhole escutcheon, c1875, 3" x 1.5". XQ/50-150

Treasury Seal knob, c1890. Other companies cast this same design. Note the fine knurled edge on this Corbin example, 2.5" dia. FF/100-300

Scales of Justice doorknob and plate from the Philadelphia City Hall, c1885. SC/300-500

Reading Hardware & The Columbian Pattern

Reading Hardware of Reading, PA, was a major manufacturer of architectural trimmings. The "Architects' Edition" of its 1899 catalog was 448 pages. There were dozens of doorknob designs and each design featured 10 or more separate items such as knobs, escutcheons, locks, latches, push buttons, letter box plates, mortise flush bolts, etc. The company also advertised offices in New York, Chicago and Philadelphia.

Reading's "Columbian" pattern was popular throughout the country. This elegant, ornate pattern was made with and without a little fox head that hides among the scrolls and foliate designs. This is a very collectible pattern.

A door plate with fox head hiding in the keyhole cover, 3" x 10".

FF/50-150

Single, grand "Columbian" pattern hinge, 6" x 6". HH/50-150

Entry knob with fox head.

FF/30-100

A pocket door pull without fox head, 7.25" x 2.25".

HH/30-100

Set of four window sash pulls with fox heads, 1.5" x 1.75".
HH/30-100

Two screen doorknobs, 1.75" dia. HH/30-100

A night latch or night works for
a mortise lock, 1" x 2.25".

HH/30-100

Mail slot with fox head (spring broken), 7" x 2.5".
HH/50-150

Mallory Wheeler

Mallory Wheeler (MW) was organized in 1834. From the beginning, it concentrated on the highest quality locks and decorative hardware. In the early 1870s, MW produced a line of solid cast bronze hardware that is equal to the designs and quality of MCCC/R&E. MW published at least one catalog and it also had an agreement with Sargent to market its product line. MW continued in business until the early 20th century and the extensive production of this company is actively sought and highly prized by collectors. Quite a few of the early knobs are dated on the shank and the early plates are nicely marked on the back.

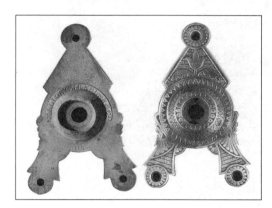

Large and dramatic triangular backplate with nice marking on reverse, c1870, 4.75" x 2.75". XQ/100-300

Passage knob with nice knurling on both the shank and the edge. XQ/50-150

Passage knob, c1880, with nice detail front and back. FF/30-100

Double-keyhole entry door plate, c1875. Marked "Mallory Wheeler & Co." 9.5" x 2.5".

HH/100-300.

Passage knob with a panel edge and compass rose design that includes Greek key, fan forms and a sunflower. c1880 XQ/30-100.

Bell pull (1.75") and backplate (5.5" x 2"),
c1875, with a good mark on reverse.

HH/100-300

Popular three-ring passage knob and plate
(6.5" x 2"), c1890 FF/30-100

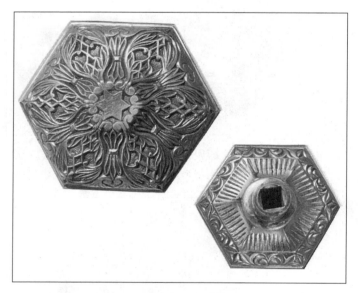

Entry-size octagonal knob in one of the most elaborate and
delicate designs of the 1870s. This knob often shows considerable wear. SQ/100-300

Large door plate in the "Arabic"
pattern, c1885, marked "M.W.
Co." 9.75" x 2.75".

HH/30-100

Round top "Arabic" pattern passage knob, c1885, with rosette. FF/under 30

Pocket door pull in the "Arabic" pattern, 2" x 4". HH/50-150

Solid cast bronze passage knob with star center and "pavilion" top. "Pat - April 14, 1874" on the shank. XQ/50-150

Recessed door pull with bees around the keyhole. SC/50-150

Yale & Towne

Linus Yale Jr. was an inventor of bank locks. In 1868, he formed The Yale Lock Manufacturing Company with Henry Towne. Unfortunately, Yale died two weeks later, so Towne took over the business. In 1883, the company name was changed to Yale & Towne and became one of America's most important hardware and lock companies. Y&T entered the 20th century by opening sales offices and factories in several foreign countries. In 1920, the company purchased several smaller hardware businesses including Sager Lock Co., and Barrows Lock Co.

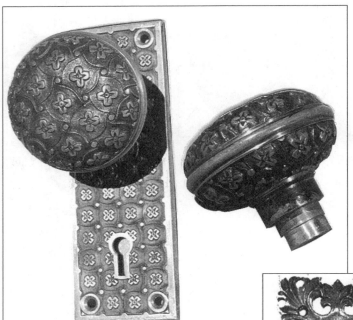

This passage knob and plate in the "Madras" pattern, c1890, is a fine example of a diaper pattern. XQ/50-150

Passage knob and plate in the "Kelp" pattern with fine rusticated design. XQ/50-150

Entry knob and plate in the "Auvergne" pattern, c1900. HH/100-300

In 1963, Y&T was purchased by the Eaton Company and the name was changed to Eaton, Yale & Towne. This company has since gone through numerous buy-outs and spin-offs and is now absorbed into Yale Security of England. Yale's 19th century hardware is frequently well marked with a Y&T inside a circular logo.

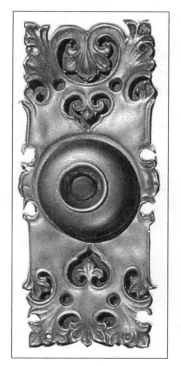

Doorbell button in the "Auvergne" pattern. XQ/50-150

Round top "Rice" pattern knob and rectangular passage door plate.

FF/30-100

Drum form passage knob in the Aesthetic taste. XQ/15-30

Sargent and the Ekado Pattern

Sargent & Co. began operations in New Haven, CT, in 1864, and quickly became one of America's major hardware companies. The company published many catalogs of high quality designs and it furnished the hardware for major building projects all across the country. Sargent & Co. remained a family-owned business until the 1960s and is still a corporate entity, although owned by a Swedish conglomerate.

The mid-1880s found Americans infatuated with decorations and designs borrowed from or influenced by Far Eastern cultures. This Aesthetic style was widely adopted by American hardware companies and Sargent patented its "Ekado" pattern in 1884. It is a great design comprised of many pieces and become one of the most popular patterns among collectors.

Concave top entry-size knob.
HH/50-150

Extra large door plate marked and dated on reverse, 2.5" x 10.75". HH/50-150

Pair of rosettes for passage knobs, 2" dia.
HH/50-150

Round top entry knob. FF/30-100

Thumb twist or night latch, marked and dated. Left is front and right is back, 1" x 2". HH/50-150

Entrance lock in working order, 2.25" x 7".

XQ/50-150

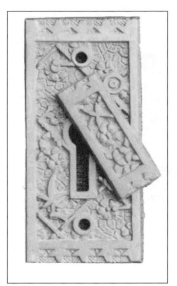

Keyhole escutcheon with swinging keyhole cover, 2.5" x 1". HH/50-150

T-handle door-bell pull, 3.25" x 2.5".

HH/50-150

Doorbell button, 2.25" dia.
HH/100-300

Single large (5.5" x 5.5") bronze hinge, marked
Sargent and dated 1885. HH/100-300

Letter slot, spring broken, 10" x 2.25". HH/100-300

Sunken center, drum form passage knob
with ribbed edge and original rosette.

HH/100-300

Branford Lock Works

Branford, from Branford, CT, published a catalog in 1886 that listed its main office and showroom at 94 Chambers St., New York. It also listed warehouse locations with Lloyd & Supplee in Philadelphia, B. Callender in Boston and S.G.B. Cook in Baltimore. Branford featured two primary designs—Oriental and Ivy—and promoted a number of special finishes. The firm is also known for several fine Neo-Grec designs and an interesting knob that has a cherub riding atop an eagle.

Double-keyhole door plate covered with Aesthetic details, c1880, 2" x 8.5". XQ/50-150

Double-keyhole cover in the Aesthetic taste, 4" x 1.75".

XQ/50-150.

Bamboo decorated entry knob with the well-known Branford "picket fence" edging, c1880. FF/30-100

Trenton

There is little information about Trenton Lock and Hardware Company other than an 1887 catalog. This was the era of Aesthetic style in America and Trenton was obviously at the forefront of producing decorative hardware in this style.

A beautiful entry knob and backplate (4.75") with shamrock motif, c1885. XQ/100-300

Passage knob with sunburst vase, flowers and diapered panels, decorated back, c1880s. FF/15-30

Hardware from Chicago

In 1878, Milton and Sidney Niles began a hardware manufacturing enterprise. They had a patent for a new type of door latching system where a knob was permanently attached to a large round shank that fit into a special lock system. This innovation was completely incompatible with the hardware of East Coast companies such as R & E and P.F. Corbin, but

the Niles built a large market for their new concept, nonetheless. In 1882, the Niles' original company was renamed "The Chicago Hardware Manufacturing Company." Over the next two decades, the company created some great hardware, including pieces for buildings designed by Louis Sullivan.

A passage size Elk's Club knob with elk head, clock and star, Sager, c1900. FF/30-100

A passage knob with multiple Aesthetic symbols. Note the Chicago-style shank, c1885. BC/15-30

Lockwood

Henry Lockwood organized his company in 1878, in Fitchburg, MA. In 1889, he purchased a major portion of Nashua Lock Company. Lockwood provided hardware for many prominent buildings, including the New York State Capital in Albany. Since 1931, The Lockwood Company has been sold several times, but has kept its corporate identity. In 1973, the company produced its 25th million lock and is presently the largest lock company in Australia.

Lockwood's "Broken Leaf" pattern of the 1880s is one of the best known American Aesthetic designs. The key image is a plant in a variety of urns; but, in another victory for popular perception over reality, it is actually a stem that is broken, rather than a leaf.

A passage knob and backplate, c1887. FF/30-100

Bell pull (1.75" dia.) and plate (3.75" x 1.5"). HH/50-150

Store door pull with fine detail, 12" x 2.25". XQ/100-300

Hopkins & Dickenson

H&D is one of the small hardware manufacturers that emerged in the 1870s to fill the growing demand for high quality cast bronze hardware. Its foundry was in Darlington, NJ, and it advertised an office and salesroom in New York City. The firm's catalogs of 1874 and another in 1879 provide an excellent pictorial review of how the plain hardware of the 1860s made a wholesale and dramatic shift to emphatic decoration by the mid-1870s.

Most of the H&D designs are strongly Neo-Grec and the quality is uniformly superior. Consequently, all H&D hardware, whether plain or fancy, is actively sought by collectors.

A recessed backplate (8.25" x 2.75") with thumb-twist knob (1.75"), c1879. HH/100-300

Combined rose and escutcheon backplate with quatrefoil, decorated paneled passage knob. SC/100-300

Triangular rosette, c1870, with strong Neo-Grec details, 4.25" x 2.25", c1879. HH/50-150

"Starburst" passage knob. XQ/30-100

Norwalk

The principal catalog of the Norwalk (CT) Lock Company is dated 1890. It shows an interesting collection of hardware that features holdover designs from the decorative 1880s and a large selection of up-to-date designs that are really quite plain. The earlier pieces are of much greater interest to collectors, several of which have terrific figural motifs. Norwalk design and casting quality is excellent, but close inspection shows how quality of material was beginning to diminish well before the turn of the century.

Fine, large door plate, c1870, with hoofed urn motif, 8" x 2.5". SQ/50-150

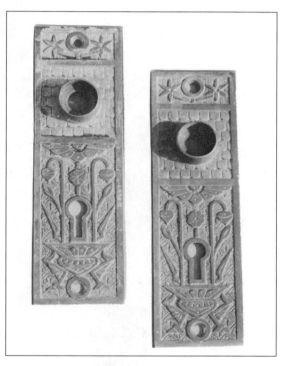

Pair of interior plates, hoofed-urn motif, 5.75" x 1.75". XQ/30-100

The so-called Bluebell knob, complete with rosette, c1885. FF/30-100

A pair of cast iron pocket door pulls in the bluebird/butterfly pattern, 8" x 3".

XQ/30-100

Passage knob in alternative pattern for the bluebird/butterfly pattern. FF/15-30

Mortise lock, double-keyhole plate, two passage knobs and night works in the popular bluebird/butterfly pattern. FF/100-300

Nashua Lock Company

In 1834, Charles Gay and Samuel Shepard formed one of America's first lock companies in Nashua, NH. In 1844, the firm produced more than 30,000 pairs of rosewood doorknobs; in 1845, Nashua earned national acclaim at an exhibition of builders hardware. After the great Boston fire of 1872, the company suffered financial problems. Nashua continued to produced great quality hardware until 1889 when it was forced to sell everything but its foundry to the Lockwood Mfg. Company. Among collectors, Nashua is especially known for store door pulls, fancy keyhole escutcheons and superior quality glass knobs of the earlier tapered shank style.

A single, straight handle pull, cast in two parts and marked "Nashua," c1880. HH/50-150

One of the very best Aesthetic door pulls you'll ever find (14.75" x 2.5"), Nashua Lock Co., c1880. HH/100-300

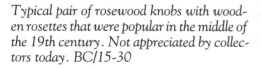

Typical pair of rosewood knobs with wooden rosettes that were popular in the middle of the 19th century. Not appreciated by collectors today. BC/15-30

Chapter 3

American Hardware in American Buildings

Ante Bellum Hardware

Hardware from the pre-Civil War decades has just begun to be researched and recorded. We know that its decoration was limited and that many different materials were used by a large number of manufacturers. Collector interest in this area is presently very low, so great things can be found at very reasonable prices. Values given here reflect a sophisticated appreciation of hardware history and design.

Pressed glass octagonal glass with polished flat top. The underside of the glass has been cut in a radiating pattern and a small star has also been cut in the top to hide the interior set screw. Attached to the original locking mechanism, c1850, which interestingly is designed to be installed very much like the modern-day "Quickset" lockset. SC/100-300

A small glass floret (2" dia.) ingeniously screwed to a brass shank by means of an internal nut which is seen through the top of the knob. This in turn is held in place with a dimpled, notched glass disc. This knob was attached to an iron shank that turned the latching mechanism by a special pivoting mechanism. SC/100-300

Pair of Sandwich-style knobs and rosettes, with original (as found) mortise lock marked "Stanley New Britain Conn," c1850. SC/500+

Sandwich-style knob in original (as found) surface mounted lock. This knob, c1850, was probably put in this c1820 lock when the house was redecorated before the Civil War. SC/300-500

The Neo-Grec Influence

Greek Revival architecture was the dominant style in America from 1820 until the Civil War, so it is not surprising that the first truly decorated hardware would feature specific motifs from Greek and Roman ruins. The palmette, anthemion, Greek key border and other strong details show up in the designs of every American hardware company of the 1870s.

The post-Civil War era was also the time when superior artistry and materials were the norm rather than the exception. This, and the ensuing building boom, resulted in a treasure-trove of cast bronze house fittings to be found and enjoyed by collectors today.

Heavy bronze entry knob, possibly an R&E variation. XQ/100-300

Bronze door lever, c1870s, 6" long. HH/30-100

A cast bronze passage knob with exceptionally thin profile and a tapered edge with egg and dart decoration. XQ/30-100

Pavilion top entry knob by Hopkins & Dickenson, c1879. Sharp detailing, including two rows of knurling. XQ/50-150

Hexagonal knob by Corbin, c1875. These knobs, which are relatively lightweight, often show considerable wear. HH/30-100

An R&E/MCCC passage knob with a sunken center with grape motif. Dated June 7, 1870 on the shank, it's one of the original MCCC designs. No marks on reverse. SC/100-300

A beautiful sunken center knob by MC-CC, 2.25", patented by R&E on June 7, 1870. Choice. SC/50-150

A fine, sunken center passage knob by Corbin, c1874. SC/50-150

Very fine wooden passage knob on a brass shank with a Neo-Grec warrior encircled by a Greek key design. HH/50-150

The Aesthetic Style In America

The Aesthetic Movement began in England as a sophisticated style that was strongly inspired by oriental cultures. In America, the English and Japanese exhibits at the Philadelphia Centennial Exhibition in 1876 were the catalysts that brought exotic, asymmetric decoration into both industrial and architectural design.

The American Aesthetic Style was the dominate decorative influence for most of the 1880s. Design elements such as sunbursts, potted plants, diagonal and chevron stripes, daisies and sunflowers were borrowed from Japan. American manufacturers also found inspiration from other exotic cultures, especially the Middle East, Egypt and even old Gothic. American companies created a huge and delicious variety of Aesthetic hardware that is actively sought by collectors today.

A slender sculpted door plate marked "Sargent," 7.25" x 2". XQ/30-100

Large rectangular door plate with urns and flowers, 8" x 2". XQ/30-100

A fine sculpted door plate, probably by Mallory Wheeler. XQ/50-100

This sculpted Aesthetic door plate by Corbin, c1885, has a passage knob that borrows Gothic influence. XQ/50-150

Fine, small knob (2+") with banded and knurled edge, probably by Branford. XQ/30-100

Flat-top Neo-Grec/Aesthetic entry knob by Sargent, c1880. XQ/30-100

Double-keyhole entry plate in the "Windsor" pattern by Reading. FF/30-100

Cast iron "Sunflower" knob by R&E, c1885. FF/15-30

An entry knob, c1880, with a design derived from Islamic calligraphy with a good R&E mark on the reverse. HH/50-150

An entry knob in the "Daylily" pattern by Sargent, c1885. Note the knurled edges.

XQ/50-150

Passage knob, c1887, with a Moorish star worked into an Aesthetic design. XQ/30-100

Gothic Revivals

Gothic design has been used in America since the 1840s and initially was more popular for country villas than churches. Authentic examples of pre-Civil War Gothic hardware are rare, but the late 19th century saw a great quantity of Gothic-inspired hardware cast in both iron and bronze.

Pointed arches, clustered columns, traceried window openings and spires encrusted with crockets and other foliate decoration are some of the key decorative elements. Most of the later Gothic hardware was designed for turn-of-the-century churches, but it is now being integrated into contemporary buildings. Much of the turn of the 20th century Gothic hardware is well cast from high quality material. It is a very popular sub-style among both beginning and advanced collectors.

A pair of large, bronze push plates with keyholes in the "Amiens" pattern by Corbin, 18.75" x 3.5". HH/100-300

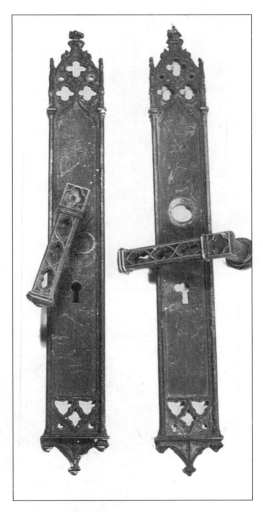

Pair of Gothic-style door handles in Monel metal marked "Yale." HH/100-300

Cast bronze passage knob with Gothic trefoil design. FF/30-100

A cast iron door pull in the "Toulon" pattern by Sargent, 13" x 3". FF/50-150

Cast bronze passage knob with tracery design like a rose window.
FF/50-150

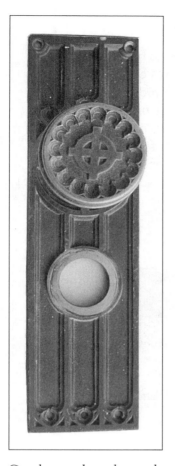

Bronze entry knob and plate, 9" x 2.75", marked "Yale." XQ/100-300

Cast bronze door plate and entry knob in the "Hendon" pattern by Yale, c1910. XQ/100-300

Passage knob in the "Cologne" pattern by Yale. SQ/50-150

Passage knob with quatrefoil design. SQ/50-150

Neo-Classical Influences

Beginning in the late-1880s, many American buildings began to turn back towards the traditional styles and forms of our nation's colonial heritage. Builders' hardware followed suit. While the design elements were still Greco/Roman in origin, they were applied with more discretion and subtlety. Hardware quality was also beginning to fall off as stamping machines and sand castings began to replace industrial artists and custom foundry work.

At the same time, commercial buildings especially were becoming larger and larger, so there was great quantities of hardware produced and are quite reasonably priced for today's collector. Study the choices and then buy only those examples that are in excellent condition.

Large (11.5" x 3.25") Neo-Classical letter slot marked "RHCo." Spring broken. FF/30-100

Unusual double doorbell plate with anthemions and egg and dart designs.

SC/50-150

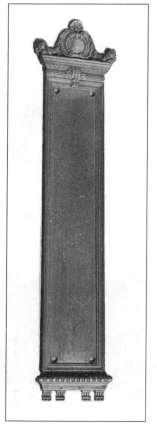

Bronze, rectangular doorbell plate with beaded edge, the "Kenwood" pattern by Reading Hardware, c1900. BC/15-30

Classically styled push plate.

XQ/30-100

Pair of Neo-Classical door plates marked "Y&T," 14" x 3". FF/50-150

Stamped brass oval bell plate with anthemions and beaded edge. BC/15-30

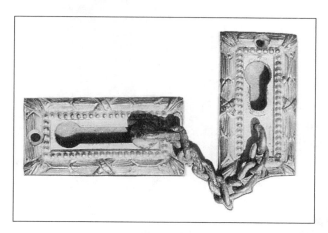

Classically styled, silver-plated chain bolt. XQ/50-150

Set of stamped metal passage plates and knobs. BC/30-100

Art Nouveau, Arts & Crafts and Art Deco

Americans had limited interest in Art Nouveau and a short but dramatic experience with Art Deco and a long and appreciative relationship with Arts & Crafts. The builders' hardware that represents each of these styles is individualistic and self-evident, but it was made in both high and low qualities. The best examples of all these styles will always hold their value.

Hand-hammered bronze entrance door plate and thumb latch. XQ/100-300

Hand-hammered bronze thumb action door plate. Note the tapered "pickets" with serrated ends, 12.5" x 3.75.

XQ/100-300

Hammered monel metal "melon" knobs with scalloped rosettes. XQ/50-150

Heavily ribbed melon-shaped entry knob in wrought steel with open-cut backplate by Earle Mfg., c1930s. XQ/30-100

Hand-hammered, heavy-gauge copper wall switch plate with dolphin designs. XQ/50-150

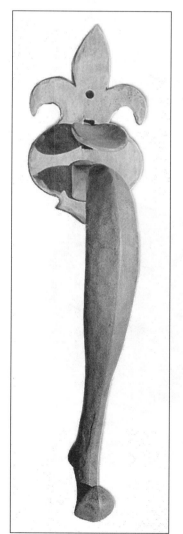

Pair of hammered monel metal, mushroom-form passage knobs with rosettes. XQ/30-100

Arts & Crafts/Neo-Classical monel metal thumb latch. BC/15-30

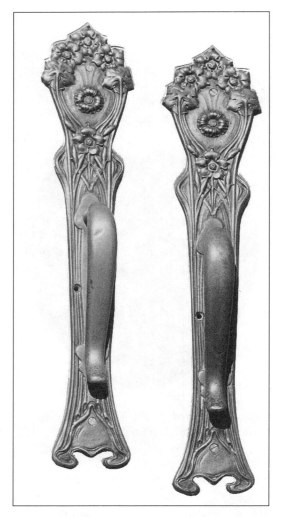

Stamped metal passage knobs and plates
(9" x 1.5") with Arts & Crafts rose motif.
BC/15-30

Pair of jumbo-sized door pulls in the "Flora"
pattern by Corbin, c1905. Strong Art Nouveau styling and large size (21" x 4.5").

SC/500+

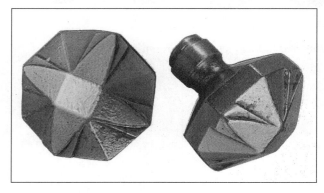

Nickel-plated Deco-style center door pull
with original backplate, 3.5" square.

BC/30-100

Nickel-plated bronze passage knob. Very deco.

FF/30-100

Chapter 4

Figural & Emblematic Hardware

Faces & Fantasies

Hardware with figural motifs is the most sought after by collectors. Hundreds of designs were created, many with classical profiles and many with faces and creatures found only the imagination of the artist. All of these examples are actively sought by collectors.

An entry-size warrior head with reeded rim decoration, c1880. SC/100-300

Copper coated, cast lead warrior head entry knob, c1860s, with original rosette. These knobs usually show wear and roughness. HH/100-300

Bronze door plate with a greenman hiding in the foliage. XQ/50-150

The "Three Feathers" Indian head passage knob, c1900. FF/100-300

Lady head entry knob from Philadelphia, c1890. Note the mushroom-footed shank. SC/100-300

Transom top door plate from a commercial or institutional building. Note the coat-of-arms and cherub face at the top and the sea serpents below. XQ/50-150

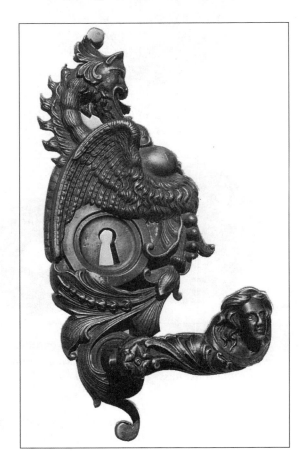

Massive, bronze, fixed handle pull, American, c1950, 13" x 6". XQ/300-500

The Cherub & Eagle passage knob by Branford Lock Works, c1885.

SC/100-300

Christopher Columbus knob and plate from a Midwestern hotel. FF/50-150

Entry knob and door plate (8.5" x 2.5") in the "Empire" pattern by Corbin, c1895.

FF/100-300

A double-keyhole door plate with dragons in the foliage. SC/100-300

The so-called "George & Martha" set is a misnomer, unless we're looking at Martha as a young girl. At any rate, it is a nice collector group, although it is invariably found in very worn condition. Both doorknobs have mushroom footed shanks, so the rosette and especially the large door plate, are hard to find. HH/300-500

Foliate & Fauna

Plant and animal forms were frequently incorporated into hardware designs of all eras. In fact, one could collect a garden full of flowers or a menagerie of little pets cast in bronze. Note that the backplates are often as ornate as the knobs themselves.

A pierce-cast entry knob with foliate design and an open back. SC/100-300

A Branford passage knob, c1890. Flower forms front and back. FF/30-100

Entry knob in the "Rococo" pattern by Corbin, c1890, features scattered flowers and shells. HH/50-150

Entry knob with broad foliate border and paneled sides. XQ/50-150

Stamped brass passage knob with leaf design.

BC/15-30

Passage knob with leaves and Aesthetic-style flowers. BC/15-30

Passage knob with floral bouquet, including wheat stalks. BC/30-100

Entry knob with American eagle motif. SC/300-500

A hummingbird passage knob by R&E, c1880.

A passage knob with three dolphins, a knurled edge and a daisy center. XQ/30-100

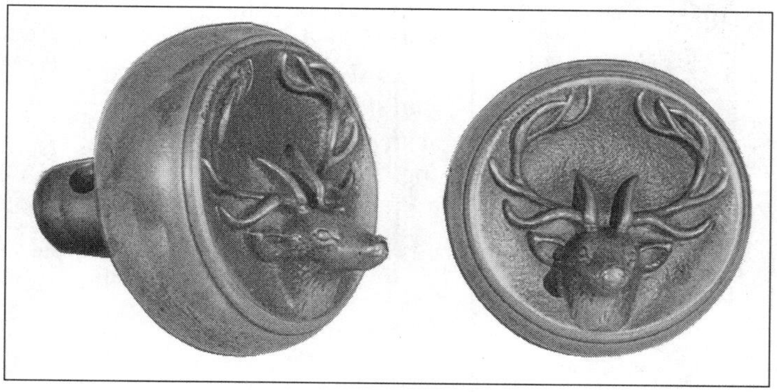

Passage knob with stag head in strong relief. SC/100-300

Seated stag entry knob cast by Corbin for the Connecticut capital, c1880s. SC/500+

Fraternal Organizations

Before TV, movies and even radio, membership in fraternal organizations was very popular, especially among men. These groups often owned their lodge building, and it was customary to install hardware specially designed for each organization. Many companies competed for this lucrative business, so there is a great variety of quality pieces to be found.

Masonic: Entrance door plate with fluted columns, Corinthian capitals and globe finials, as well as a coat-of-arms and masonic symbols. The doorknob has a six-pointed and sloping border with anthemion desing. SC/300-500

Masonic: Entrance door plate. The doorknob has a five-pointed star and laurel leaf border. SC/300-500

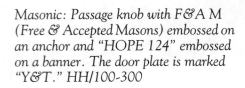

Masonic: Passage knob with F&A M (Free & Accepted Masons) embossed on an anchor and "HOPE 124" embossed on a banner. The door plate is marked "Y&T." HH/100-300

Masonic: Entry knob with Masonic emblem and knurled edge. HH/30-10

Masonic: Nickel-plated doorknocker/peephole from the Order of the Eastern Star. HH/50-150

Masonic: 20th century brass Masonic doorknocker/peep-hole combination. HH/50-100

Elks: A passage knob with clock and B.P.O.E. (Benevolent Protective Order of Elks). FF/30-100

Elks: Entrance door plate and knob from an Elks Lodge. Plate (12.75" x 3.25") is marked "Darcy" and includes a strongly embossed elk head and the number 14. HH/100-300

Elks: Passage knob with elk, clock and star, by Sager. HH/50-150

Nickel-plated Odd Fellows passage knob with beaded rim. FF/30-100

Odd Fellows: Bronze passage knob with the three rings filled with F-L-T (Faith, Love and Truth). FF/30-100

Odd Fellows: Nickel-plated peephole cast with satyr faces and fraternal emblems. HH/50-150

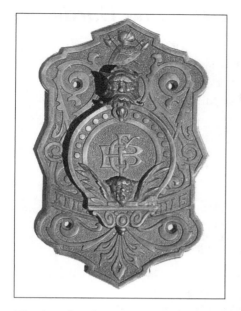

Knights of Pythias: Bronze peephole in the same pattern as the Odd Fellows, 7" x 4.25". HH/50-150

Knights of Pythias: Entry knob from a lodge in Indiana. Plate (11" x 2.5") is the Oproto design by Y&T.

HH/50-150

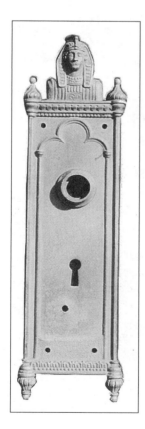

Shriners: Door plate with pharaoh head and Moorish arch, missing a cast camel that covered the three holes at the bottom. SC/100-300

Shriners: Bronze entry knob made into a paperweight and marked Corbin.

XQ/100-300

Government, Commercial & Institutional Hardware

In the decades before and after 1900, all levels of government also built impressive buildings, and sought specially designed door and window fittings. Somewhere there exists the seal of each state on a doorknob, as well as untold examples of beautifully crafted organizational symbols and insignia.

Entry knob with the Seal of New Haven County. HH/50-150

Entry knob with the Pennsylvania State Seal. HH/50-150

Entry knob and plate (11" x 3.5") from the Cook County Courthouse, Chicago. Classical design and detail, with the county seal cast at the bottom. XQ/50-150

Oval entry knob from the Massachusetts State House. HH/50-150

Entry knob with a steamboat motif, the Seal of St. Louis set within receding concentric circles. SC/100-300

A cast iron YMCA passage knob. BC/15-30

Passage knob from a Lowe's Theatre. BC/15-30

Passage knob with a sailing ship from a Boston bank. SC/100-300

Entry knob and rosette that features a standing lion and wreath from a Chicago hotel. BC/15-30

111

Crown center entry knob from a Canadian bank. SC/100-300

"Slyvania" means "light" and was a popular name for homes, hotels and resorts. BC/15-30

Passage knob and plate (9" x 3") from the B&O Railroad Station in Baltimore. HH/50-150

A bronze YWCA passage knob. Several companies made these knobs over many years. BC/15-30

Public School Knobs

Doorknob collectors are always meeting people who remember fancy knobs on high school doors. School knobs were made in great quantity by several companies and preserve a lot of history for very reasonable prices.

The Chicago Board of Education passage knob features a hand, a torch and laurel leaves. FF/30-100

Octagonal NYC Board of Education passage knob and lock. All brass. FF/30-100

Passage knob from the Newark, NJ, Board of Education. FF/30-100

Detroit Board of Education passage knob. FF/30-100

New York City Public School oval passage knob. FF/15-30

Reading, PA, Board of Education. Nice scholastic scene. SC/100-300

Calligraphic

The late 19th century was an era when good writing skills were admired and a lot of commercial promotion focused on fancy lettering and calligraphic designs. Individuals, as well as institutions, ordered their initials or logos in cast bronze. The result is a vast variety of calligraphic hardware now available to collectors.

A "Double H" passage knob, probably made for an 1890s hotel. BC/15-30

The "WU" passage knob may have come from Washington University. BC/15-30

A passage knob that presents the circle in body, form and spirit. XQ/30-100

Nickel-plated passage knob from the Jefferson Hotel. BC/15-30

"SHS" monogram in great rusticated calligraphy, 2.5". BC/15-30

Heavy bronze passage knob with knurled edge and typical Corbin details, c1875. XQ/50-150

Bronze passage knob from the Lehigh & Wilkes Barre Coal Company.

XQ/50-150

"WDG" monogram in cast iron. BC/15-30

The Hanna Caldwell Doorknob

Mrs. Hanna Caldwell was the wife of a minister who served with George Washington's Army. In 1780, she was shot by a British Soldier as she stood on the porch of her husband's parsonage. This tragedy inspired Americans at the ensuing battle of Elizabethtown, NJ, and the incident was later incorporated into the Seal of Union County, NJ.

This Hanna Caldwell doorknob dates from around 1900.

SC/300-500

The John Wannamaker Story

"…The plumb of honor, the level of truth and the square of integrity…" That was the focus and creed of Philadelphia merchant John Wannamaker, and he built these principles into a great merchandising empire, while changing the face of American retail shopping.

Before Wannamaker opened his first store in 1861—a men's clothing shop located on the site of George Washington's Philadelphia home—America's Main Street was just a series of small, one or two item stores where customers had to haggle over prices and guarantees were few and far between. Wannamaker's first day receipts were $24.67, of which he reinvested $24 in his business and his dreams. In 1876, he moved to The Grand Depot, an abandoned railroad shed across from City Hall. By 1885 he had become the first store to be lighted by electricity—and had recorded his first $1 million sales day.

John Wannamaker continued to build on his vision of a new way to sell. He was totally customer oriented and was the first retailer to bring a broad variety of items together under one roof. He instituted uniform quantity and specific pricing and established a no-questions-asked return policy. He also invented the "White Sale," which has become a January tradition.

In 1902, Wannamaker's business had grown to where he began a major expansion project. He kept his Grand Depot open throughout a mammoth three-stage building program that lasted until 1911. When the project was complete, there stood a 12 story Roman-Doric "Merchants cathedral" that rose 247 feet and enclosed 2 million square feet of floor space.

At the dedication of his flagship store, there were 35,000 guests, including President Taft and a special greeting from the Emperor and Empress of Japan. The crowds came to browse, to shop and to see the huge, 2,500-pound bronze eagle that Wannamaker had bought at the Louisiana Purchase Exposition in 1904. They were also treated to a concert from the Wannamaker organ, also purchased in New Orleans, which soon became the world's largest, with 451 stops and 30,067 pipes and which would play every business day thereafter.

John Wannamaker died in 1922, by which time he presided over a retail empire that included more than a dozen stores both in the United States and overseas. His vision, his determination and his belief in building trust and satisfaction with his customers made him one of the great entrepreneurs who lived—and created—the American Dream.

In 1904, when Wannamaker was deep into his mammoth store expansion, he ordered special hardware to commemorate the history he knew he was making. The knob and plate pictured here were removed from that flagship store in 1985.
SC/100-300

Chapter 5

Hardware for Doors

Decorative Mortise Locks & Strikes

Well before 1850, the mortise lock had supplanted the surface-mounted "box" lock in most American construction. Initially, these locks had plain brass fronts, but, as decorative hardware became popular, this part of the lock was cast with a pattern that matched the knob and rosette. In general, even though many mortise locks are of superior design and decoration, they are presently of low interest to collectors. Examples of early door locks are shown in Chapter 3 where Ante Bellum hardware is discussed.

A typical passage lock set with decorative mortise lock matching the door plates and doorknobs. Maker's logo "PLCo" embossed on side plate. Lock only BC/15-30; entire set.

XQ/50-150

A mortise lock with the R&E logo and a front plate cast with an Aesthetic design of potted flowers. Note the sunflower around the upper screw hole. XQ/30-100

Two Aesthetic-style strike plates, both with lotus flowers and one with a bumblebee. XQ/30-100.

Door Handles & Pulls

Commercial buildings and large residences often used handles and pulls instead of doorknobs. Door handles of the 1860s and 1870s often had figural motifs and were cast from heavy bronze. Around 1880, door handles began using thinner backplates, but the designs were very detailed. Around 1890, the heavier style came back into favor. Always check the thumb-latch; it is often missing or replaced, but sometimes there is maker's mark and date underneath.

Superb pair of thumb latch door pulls, 20" x 3.25", plates with 8" handles. Exquisite detail and beautiful color.

SC/500+

Massive bronze door pull, 26" x 3.5", c1890. Note the ribbon design of the handle and the exceptionally ornate casting.

SC/300-500

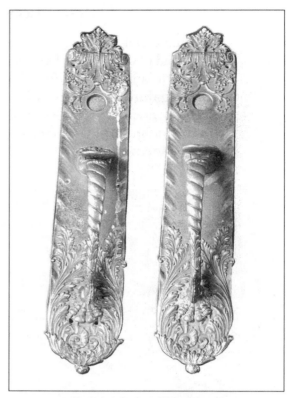

An oversized set of door pulls in the "Veroccio"
pattern by R&E, 18.5" long x 3.25" wide. SC/
100-300

Cast bronze door pull in
the Moorish style, 15" x
3.5". HH/50-150

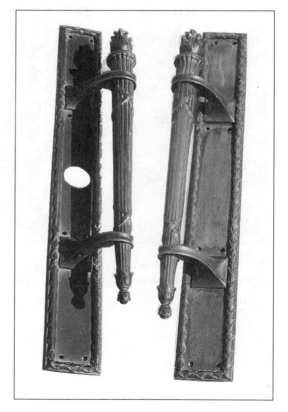

Pair of heavy brass handles and plates, 12" x 3.5".
BC-30-100

Pair of torch handle door pulls,
18" x 3". HH/500+

120

Keyhole Escutcheons

Considering how many keyhole escutcheons have been found, it sometimes seems that every house had a different one on every door. Because of this quantity—and variety—these little door fittings are great fun to collect. Look for the early ones with side-by-side double keyholes and those that have faces or animals on the swing cover. Another hint: learn how to tell whether the swing cover is missing.

Large copper-clad cast lead double-keyhole escutcheon, 4.5" x 2.25", in the Neo-Grec style of the early 1870s.

SC/50-150

Neo-grec keyhole escutcheon with Irish setter cast onto keyhole cover, 4.25" x 1.5". SC/100-300

Single keyhole escutcheon by MCCC/R&E, dated June 6, 1870. Coinage-quality casting, 4" x 2.5". SC/100-300

Copper-coated cast lead keyhole escutcheon
with warrior head on cover, c1870, 1.75"
x 2.75". HH/30-100

Copper-plated lead keyhole
escutcheon with female profile. Corbin, 1874-75.

HH/30-100

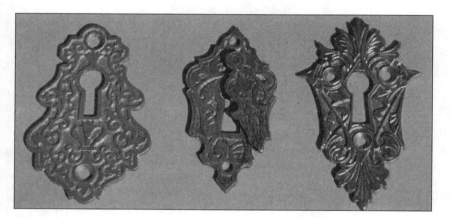

Group of three keyhole escutcheons from the 1870s, one with keyhole cover.
FF/30-100 for all three

Neo-grec keyhole escutcheon by
Corbin, 1874-75. FF/15-30

Cast bronze tapered keyhole escutcheon, probably by Y&T, c1870s, 3.5" x 2.5. HH/30-100

Very large brass double keyhole, c1860, 3.75" x 2.25". HH/15-30

White porcelain double-keyhole escutcheon, with keyhole cover, c1860, 4" x 2.25". HH/30-1005-20. White porcelain double-keyhole escutcheon, without keyhole cover, c1860, 3.5" x 1". HH/15-30

A passage door keyhole escutcheon by Mallory-Wheeler, c1875, 1" x 2". HH/15-30

Composition keyhole escutcheon, 2.5", from the early
1870s. HH/15-30

Group of Aesthetic-style keyhole escutcheons. BC/30-100 for all

Group of covered keyhole escutcheons and
thumb twists in the "Woburn" pattern by
Y&T, c1910. BC/50-150 for all

Silver-plated double-keyhole
escutcheon with decorated
cover plate, c1870, 1.75" x
1.75". HH/50-150

Door Plates

Every doorknob was designed with a complimentary door plate or rosette, but often the pieces are not found together on an old door, or the proper pieces are separated after they are removed. Therefore, door plates themselves are very collectible and can be just as interesting and impressive as doorknobs. Often, the swinging keyhole cover is missing and this can affect the price considerably.

Plates with two keyholes were used on entrance doors; one key was for daytime in-and-out while large, covered "master keyhole" was for operating the heavy security bolt. By the end of the 19th century, the cylinder lock had come into use, so many door plates have a large hole cast in the upper part and this provides a good clue to relative age.

The decorative ferrule around the doorknob spindle hole is often the same design as the rosette used on passage doors. Thus, some door plates are sometimes described as a "combined rose and escutcheon."

La Grande entry plate from Reading Hardware, c1899. HH/30-100

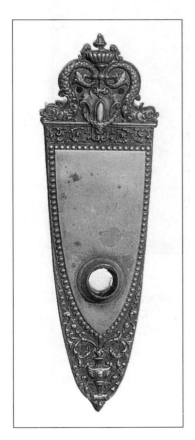

Entry door plate in the "Certosa" pattern by Yale & Towne, c1910. Note the aqua-critters, the cherub face and a coat of arms, 16.25" x 3.5". HH/50-150

Entry plate with finely detailed foliate design. XQ/30-100

Gilded, Neo-Classical entry door plate from an important commercial building. Marked "Y&T" on the reverse, 15.5" x 3.5".

SC/100-300

Rococo style entry door plate, originally silver-plated.

XQ/50-150

From left: Cast bronze double-keyhole plate c1890, BC/15-30; stamped brass entry door plate, c1895, BC/15-30; stamped brass passage door plate, the "Roanoke" pattern by Corbin, c1895.

BC/15-30

Double-keyhole door plate with seven different flowers cast into the design, 7.25" x 2".

FF/30-100

Aesthetic style double-keyhole entry plate by Sargent, except that only one keyhole was ever cast into this example.
XQ/30-100

Cast bronze Neo-Grec backplate by Corbin, c1875. This design was also used for Corbin's enameled hardware, 2.5" x 7".
SC/100-300

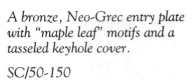

A bronze, Neo-Grec entry plate
with "maple leaf" motifs and a
tasseled keyhole cover.

SC/50-150

Bronze, Neo-Grec backplate by
R&E, c1870, 5" x 2".

SC/100-300

A bronze, Neo-Grec
double-keyhole entry
plate by H&D,
c1870. 7.5" x 2.5".
SC/100-300

Single keyhole entry plate by
H&D in the Neo-Grec taste;
note the missing swing cover,
7.5" x 2". SC/50-150

Neo-grec "crown top" triangular backplate by H&D, 3.75" x 2.5". SC/50-150

Double-keyhole Neo-Grec entry door plate by H&D, c1879. 7.5" x 2".

SC/100-300

A triangular backplate by R&E, c1870, made for an octagonal knob. SC/50-150

*Highly stylized triangular backplate, c1870,
2.5" x 4.5". SC/100-300*

*Long, narrow Neo-Grec
backplate from R&E with
lion face keyhole cover. This
cover was upside down when
the plate was removed from
the door. SC/50-150*

*Neo-grec triangular backplate from Corbin
c1874, 2.5" x 4.5". SC/50-150*

Bells, Buttons, Pulls & Cranks

Doorbells and bell parts make up a separate area of hardware collecting. Many, many styles and varieties can be found from 1840-1920. After looking at many doorbell systems in situ, it is apparent that quite often various parts were mixed, matched and jury-rigged by homeowners. Therefore, this book presents these pieces by separate function, and if you wish to install an "authentic" working bell, you can combine various pieces, as well.

T-handle bell lever, c1870s, dog holding a bone. SC/300-500

Wall mount doorbell marked "Abbe's," c1860s. FF/50-150

A 3.5" dia. crank-activated doorbell by Corbin, c1870s. FF/50-150

A 4" lever action door-bell with fancy cover. XQ/50-150

A 3.5" dia. pull-action doorbell marked "C. Penfield 1870" on the bell and "Turnbull Pat'd June 13, 1865…May 18, 1869" on base. Note the little pulley that smoothes the action of the pull chain. HH/100-300

Cast iron doorbell with great Aesthetic motifs including an owl, stork, crane and various plant forms. Note the sunflower center. HH/100-300

*Fancy 4.5" dia. pull-action doorbell dated 1879.
FF/100-300*

*Very fancy 4" dia. nickel-plat-
ed brass doorbell, note the
missing tab. HH/100-300*

*Pull-action doorbell, 4"
dia., strong Aesthetic
details. FF/50-150*

Plain brass, 5.75" pull-action door-bell by Corbin, patented Dec. 30, 1879. BC/30-100

Cast brass clock-works doorbell, 4.25" dia., c1900, thumb twist action.

BC/50-150

Cast brass thumb twist clockworks doorbell, 4.5" dia., marked "R&E Mfg. Co. Pat. Aug 1, 93." HH/100-300

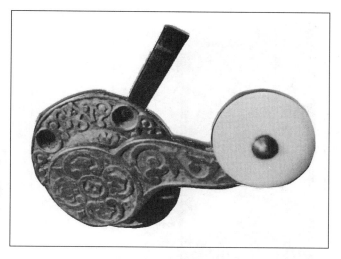

Cast bronze doorbell crank with porcelain knob, 3.5" handle, 1.75" dia. plate. HH/30-100

Cast bronze doorbell crank with bronze knob, 3.5" handle, 1.75" knob. HH/30-100

Fancy cast bronze thumb twist with 3" stamped brass backplate, c1880s. XQ/30-100

*Cast bronze thumb twist and plate.
FF/30-100*

*Cast bronze thumb twist and back-
plate, 3.5", c1900. FF/15-30*

*Oval, stamped brass bell thumb
twist, 5.5" x 2", c1890.*

FF/15-30

*Cast plate with instruction on how to operate the bell
(says "TURN"), c1890s. FF/15-30*

Large circular doorbell button, 3.5" dia., c1900. BC/15-30

Doorbell button cover, c1880. BC/15-30

Diamond-shaped doorbell button, 3" x 2", nickel-plated brass and mother-of-pearl.

XQ/15-30

Classically styled doorbell button, 2.5" dia., rope-twist edge. BC/15-30

Cast bronze doorbell plate, 6.25" x 2.25", "Altena" pattern by RHCo., c1910. XQ/30-100

Fancy doorbell backplate, 5" x 2.5, c1890. XQ/30-100

Cast bronze Neo-Classical doorbell button plate, 6" x 2.25", the "Toulon" pattern by Reading. XQ/50-150

Doorbell button in the "Verdun" pattern by RHCo., c1900, features a strong fleur-de-lis pattern, 6.75" x 2.75". FF/30-100

Doorbell button in the "Portulaca" pattern by Penn Hardware, c1907. Note the stylized dolphins, 4" x 1.5". FF/30-100

Cast bronze doorbell button plate marked "JFW," c1880s, 5" x 1.5".

XQ/15-30

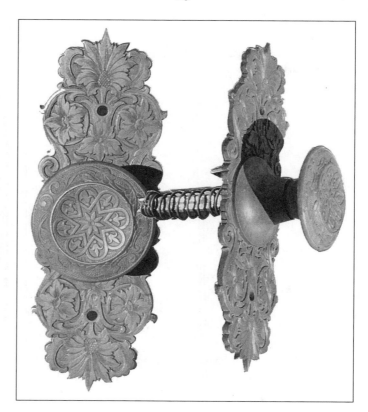

Doorbell pull, 2" dia., floral backplate by R&E, c1872. Coinage quality casting.

SC/100-300

Mercury glass doorbell pull with iron shank and screw-in rosette. HH/30-100

A tapered shank, cut glass doorbell pull, c1880s, 1.75" wide. HH/30-100

Doorbell backplate made for a doctor's office, c1880, 4.5" x 2.25". HH/50-150

Bronze doorbell pull and backplate, note that the designs do not match, c1875, 1.75" x 3.5". FF/30-100

Doorbell knob, 2" dia., c1880. HH/30-100

Pull-down Aesthetic style T-lever, 5" x 2.75", by Sargent, c1870s. HH/50-150

Cast bronze thumb-action bell lever.
Marked "Pat. Jan 23, 1877."

HH/30-100

*Bronze T-handle bell lever, c1870s, 6" x
2.75". HH/30-100*

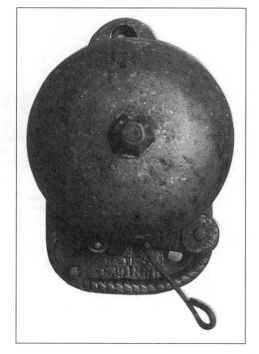

*Wall mount, lever action doorbell,
dated 1866, plate is 4.5", bell is 3"
dia. FF/50-150*

Aesthetic-style T-handle doorbell lever with a bluebird. XQ/100-300

Cast bronze Neo-Grec T-lever bell pull with porcelain knob. HH/30-100

An early hardware sample board, c1860, in "as found" condition. Three different T-handles, two pulls and an unusual spindle-activated bell system. HH/100-300

A doorbell/doorknob combination. There are different styles of this concept. HH/50-150

A solid brass doorbell marked "Russell & Erwin...1890..." with a thumb twist that winds a clock spring. An exterior bell pull would activate the ringer. Other varieties of this concept can be found, 4.75" dia. HH/50-150

Unusual doorbell marked "Pierce's Electic [sic] Bell Pat Dec 10 82" and "Bell M'F'G' Co. Omaha & P.B.&W. Co. N.Y." This bell works with unusual spring and plunger mechanism. SC/100-300

Mail Slots

When the postman used to walk door to door and written letter was the preferred means of communication, everyone needed a mail slot in their front door. Today, most of these fittings are too small to handle fat magazines and junk mail and they are not easily secured, so there is little demand in the renovation market. When buying a mail slot, look for the BIG ones and be sure the spring is still operable. Also remember that if you plan to install it, there was an inside liner and plate that was usually very plain and therefore was almost never saved and is now very hard to locate.

Bronze LETTERS slot, c1880s, with a bluebird and acorn motif, 8" x 3". XQ/50-150

Bronze LETTERS slot with Chinese Chippendale decoration, 3" x 5". FF/30-100

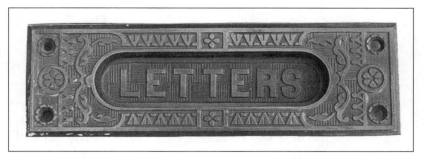

Aesthetic-style LETTERS slot, 7.25" x 2.25", valued at $40.

Combination electric bell/mail slot,
5.5" x 3.25". SC/50-150

Neo-grec LETTERS slot,
bronze, 8" x 3". FF/30-100

Large MAIL slot (9" x 3") in Monel metal. HH/30-100

Bronze PAPERS slot, 11" x
4", c1870s. HH/100-300

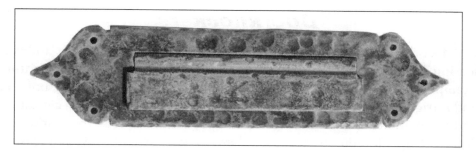

Monel metal mail slot, 11" x 2.75". BC/15-30

Bronze LETTERS slot in the so-called "Starfish" pattern, 7.5" x 2.75". HH/50-150

Unusual combination mail slot and doorbell. Here shown incomplete. SC/50-150

Bronze LETTERS slot from the John Hancock building, 12" x 3". HH/50-150

Doorknockers

Doorknockers are another separate area of hardware interest and collecting. Many of the authentic, hand-wrought 18th- and early-19th century examples sell for hundreds or even thousands. There were many unusual and intriguing knockers designed in the later 19th and early 20th centuries, and the real ones can also bring big money. Unfortunately, the market today is filled with reproductions, so it hard to find the real thing at a reasonable price. The pieces shown here are authentic but not particularly high powered. They represent what can be found that is functional and affordable.

Miniature or interior doorknockers: These were cast in brass and iron and are found in many different styles. This is a separate area of collecting and some examples can sell for several hundred dollars. The examples shown here are 3" to 4" long and date mostly from the 20th century.

Bronze knocker with Art Nouveau lines, 3.75" x 7.25". BC/30-100

Bronze doorknocker with oval backplate, 20th century, 6" x 3". BC/30-100

Late 19th century figural bronze knocker. Some wear, missing strike, 6.75" x 3.75". BC/30-100

Small brass knocker, early-19th century, from a Philadelphia townhouse, 6" x 3". BC/30-100

Aladdin Homes gave away these door-knockers as Christmas presents in 1926, 6" long. HH/30-100

Hand-wrought brass knocker, c1900. HH/30-100

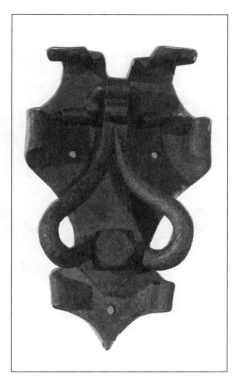

Wrought iron knocker in the Arts & Crafts style, 4.5" x 7.5". BC/30-100

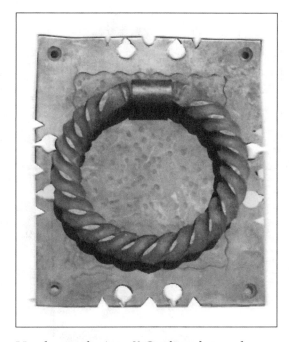

Hand-wrought Arts & Crafts style iron door-knocker. BC/30-100

Wrought iron, rope twist door-knocker, 7.5" x 5.5", missing strike. BC/30-100

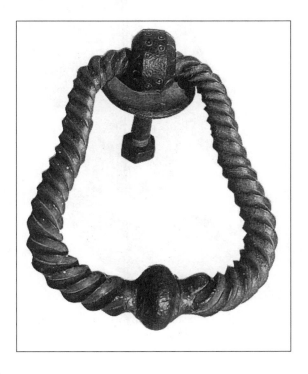

Turn-of-the-century hand-forged iron doorknocker.
BC/30-100

Large open-work cast iron plate with brass knocker, 20th century, 13" x 6".

BC/30-100

Cast iron doorknocker in the form a dog head, with old brown paint. HH/100-300

Late-18th or early-19th century hand-wrought iron doorknocker, 12" x 10". SC/500+

Miniature doorknocker: Classic style.

Miniature doorknocker: Fist holding swing arm.

Miniature doorknocker: Galleon in full sail.

Miniature doorknocker: Coat of Arms.

Miniature doorknocker: Lion head.

Hinges

The large homes and commercial buildings of the late 19th century had large doors that required very large and sometimes massive hinges. Even though they were unseen most of the time (because the door is closed) the industrial artists of the time didn't hesitate to make them as ornate and beautiful as the knobs, plates and keyhole covers.

Many of the large homes had high, thick baseboard moldings, so the hinges were designed to swing the door out while it opened. This meant that an inch or more of the hinge would be exposed when the door was closed and this portion of the back of each leaf was also embossed and trimmed with fancy finials at the ends of the pins.

Few doors today can use these beautiful, heavy bronze hinges, so they are often found at bargain prices. If you plan to use vintage hinges, be sure to check if they are pintel type; if so, be sure to buy all lefts or all rights.

Pintel hinge, 4.5" x 4.5", with both Aesthetic & Art Nouveau motifs. Note the sunflowers sculpted around the screw holes. HH/30-100

Pair of very Aesthetic hinges with knurled finials, 4" x 4". FF/30-100

Single hinge in the Aesthetic taste, marked "F.C. Linde" on reverse, 4.5" x 4.5". XQ/30-100

Pair of small tufted hinges by Corbin, c1890, 3.5" x 3.5". FF/30-100

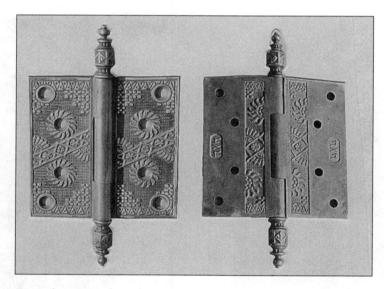

Pair of very Aesthetic hinges, 4" x 4". HH/50-150

Large hinge from a court-house or government building, 6" x 7". SC/50-150

*Pair of fancy pin type hinges by Hopkins & Dickenson,
c1879, 5" x 7". HH/30-100*

*Fancy iron hinge, c1890, 3.5" x 3.5".
BC/15-30*

*A heavy bronze single hinge, Greek Revival design, probably from the 1860s, 5" x 7".
XQ/30-100*

157

Pair of MCCC/R&E bronze hinges, 5" x 5", pat. June 8, 1869. XQ/50-150

Pair of pintel style hinges, 4.5" x 4.5", dated Jan. 18, 1870. XQ/50-150

Pair of fancy pintel type hinges, 5" x 5", steeple style finials and lotus flower motif; $45 for the pair.

Fancy single large hinge, 5" x 7". XQ/30-100

Small hinge with faces on both leaf plates and double lion heads on the post finials, 3.5" x 3.5". HH/50-150

Pocket Door Hardware

Pocket doors are another architectural feature found primarily in 19th century houses. The special hardware used on these doors is therefore one of those items that is hard to find if you need it, but is of minimal interest to others. Some of the recessed pulls or flush plates are popular among collectors because they are highly decorated. If you are buying pocket door mortise locks for re-use, make sure they function properly; very often they are inoperable and missing important internal pieces.

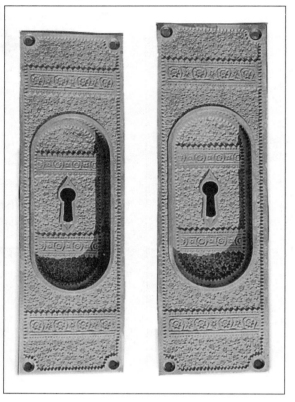

Pair of strongly Aesthetic, recessed pulls, 5.75" x 2.25". XQ/30-100

Pair of large recessed pulls, 8" x 2.5", marked "Design Pat. Jan. 8, 84." XQ/50-150

A set of pocket door mortise locks, 8" x 4", and four matching recessed pulls, 2" x 4". Original design by Norwich, c1885, but this pattern may have been "borrowed" by F.C. Lind, Cresskill, NJ. FF/50-150

Push Plates

Push plates can be found in many sizes, styles and levels of quality. They are popular among both collectors and home decorators and show up often in the antique hardware market. They were also popular as an advertising medium.

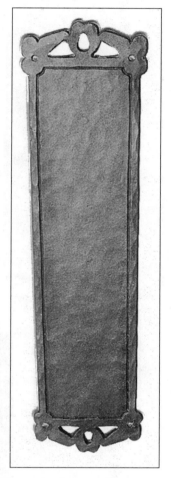

Massive bronze PUSH plate in the "Windsor" pattern by Sargent, 16" x 4", c1885. HH/50-150

Fancy bronze push plate with Elizabethan strap-work decoration, 16" x 3.5". HH/30-100

Arts & Crafts style brushed and hammered iron push plate, 3.5" x 3". BC/15-30

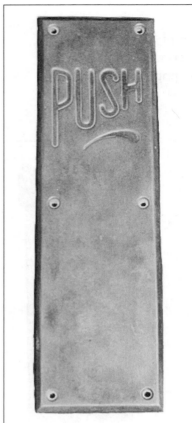

A heavy bronze plate with PUSH scripted into the top, 12" x 3.5". HH/30-100

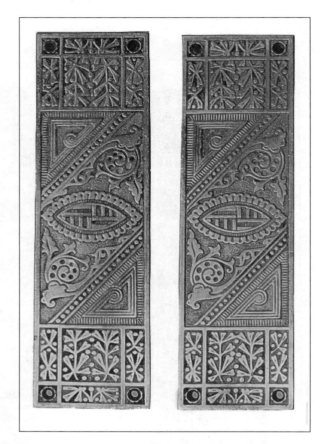

Pair of bronze push plates by Corbin, c1890, 9.25" x 2.75". HH/100-300

A fine, crisp set of push plates in the Aesthetic taste. HH/100-300

Store Door Handles

Store door handles derive their name from the fact that these are the typical hardware found on the Main Street establishments of the 1870s and 1880s. They generally have thin backplates that are highly decorated and a fancy handle and thumb latch. Often they were cast in two pieces and they show up as singles and in pairs. Make sure the plates are not bent or damaged and that the thumb latch is original. Because of the heavy store traffic, many of these handles show considerable wear and this lowers their value for collectors.

Grand, two-piece door pull by R&E, with superb style and decorative detail. SC/100-200

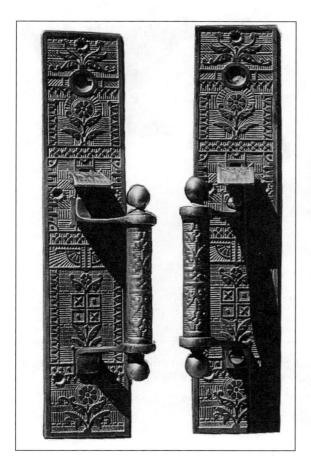

A fine pair of door handles marked "Sargent & Co.", note the nice Aesthetic sunflower motif, c1885, 12.5" x 2.5". XQ/50-150

Two-piece bronze "Bird of Paradise" door handle. SC/ 100-300

Figural door handle and thumb latch with flora, fauna, a pagoda top and a tasseled bottom. SC/100-300

Large Aesthetic-style door pull by Sargent, with patent date of 1880 cast under the thumb latch, 7.5" x 2.75". SC/100-300

Bronze door pull with matching lock, c1870. XQ/30-100

French Style Hardware

There is a lot of "French" hardware in America. Much of it has been imported, but much of it has also been manufactured by American companies. The best way to tell is to check the spindle: the large size is American; the small size in the import. It is typical to find French hardware with a gold wash over the bronze. Even when some of this wears off, it creates a rich, mellow surface. The French style is easy to identify and many pieces have excellent figural details in the designs.

Figural French doorknob in the form of a Hindu head, 3.25" long. SC/50-150

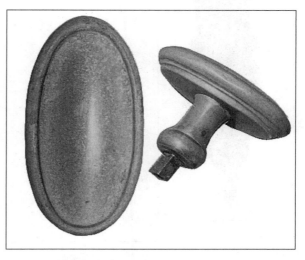

Oval knob with a molded top, step-down back and unusual round footed shank, 3", c1900. BC/15-30

Small bronze knob and rosette from a turn-of-the-century Newport mansion, 2". XQ/50-150

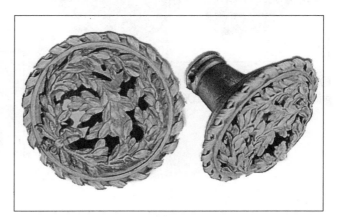

Small bronze French knob with open wreath and reticulated border. The top unscrews and colored fabric is set behind the openwork, 2.25" dia. SC/100-300

French-style backplate marked "Dandois."
FF/30-100

Figural door bolt handle with fancy gearbox.
SC/50-150

Oval passage knob with concentric design,
2.5". BC/15-30

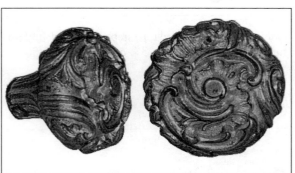

Ornate passage knob in the French style with original
gilding, 2.25". BC/30-100

Very unusual, lozenge-shape French
doorknob with flowers, ribbons, torch and
finial, 2.5" long, valued at $30.

Heavy oval knob with twisted and beaded edging, 2.5" long.

XQ/15-30

Oval knob with floral motifs, finished in gold wash, 2.5" long.

XQ/15-30

Pair of door bolt knobs and gearboxes, marked "Y&T."
BC/30-100

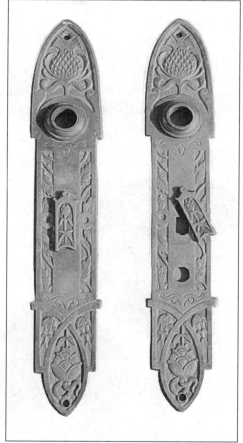

Pair of Art Nouveau-style bronze door plates with covered keyholes and thistle design. XQ/50-150

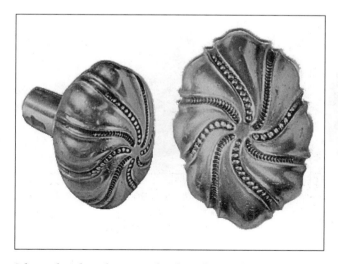

Silver-plated oval passage knob with spiral motif, 2.75" long. SC/50-150

Chapter 6

Clear Glass Doorknobs

Tapered Shank Style

The first patent for applying a glass knob to a metal shank was awarded in 1837. These very early knobs have not been well researched nor identified, but it is likely that most of the earliest variety used straight iron shanks. By the 1860s, the typical glass doorknob was set into a tapered, stepped back, brass shank that was machine rolled around the base of the knob. Molten lead was then forced into the space between glass and metal to form a non-slip connection. Many tapered shanks in iron are also found, and these probably pre-date the brass ones.

Tapered shank knobs use a thin, wafer-like rosette which is generally interchangeable between knob patterns, but these are often missing and are hard to find.

Entry sized knob, pressed to simulate punted glass, narrow waist and crisscross foil center. FF/30-100

Press-faceted passage knob on brass shank. FF/15-30

Flat-top octagon passage knob with paneled sides and molded back, on short pedestal base, crisscross foil, iron shank. HH/30-100

Pressed passage knob with drawn waist and sharply cast plateau top, on a single step-brass shank, crisscross foil interior. FF/15-30

Passage knob with pinched and paneled waist, kneaded octagon form, on iron shank. FF/15-30

Entry-size rounded octagon with pedestal waist, brass shank and nice solarized color. HH/30-100

Pressed, square-edged octagon with flat top, crisscross center and brass shank. BC/15-30

Controlled bubble
knob in elongated
mushroom form, ta-
pered brass shank,
3.25".

SC/100-300

Pressed rounded octagon with raised
top, crisscross center and brass shank.
FF/15-30

Flat-top, rounded octagon entry knob, iron shank
and crisscross center. HH/30-100

Pressed glass passage knob, 1860s, drawn waist,
multi-step brass shank, rounded octagon with flat top
and plain foil interior. BC/15-30

Cut and polished knob jumbo with tapered
brass shank. SC/100-300

Mercury Glass

In 1834, the Boston Silver Glass Company advertised both cut and pressed glass knobs. In the 1850s, several catalogs showed hollow glass knobs that were silvered inside. This "mercury" glass was really a coating of the same silver nitrate that was used on blown glass Christmas tree ornaments. These silvered glass knobs were made in several interesting varieties and were popular in America up through the 1870s.

The silver coating will often flake off because of moisture gathering inside the knob, so note that most collectors are only looking for examples in excellent condition.

An interesting doorknob set showing American ingenuity and workmanship in doorknob construction. These knobs have threaded shanks and an interesting spindle system. Note the large stamped brass rosettes. SC/100-300

Mercury glass knob on a mushroom footed "pedestal" shank, complete with original rosette. SC/50-150

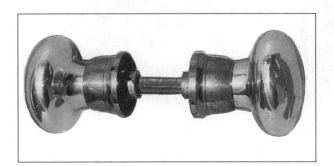

Pair of passage-size mercury knobs with early shanks. FF/30-100

Entry-size mercury knob with early tapered shank. HH/30-100

Passage size mercury knob on pewter shank with original pewter rose that is dated 1869 and 72. HH/50-150

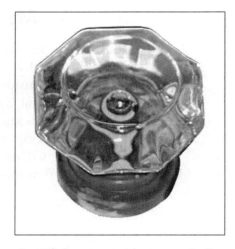

Rounded octagon with mercury bullet center, raised top and red brass shank. FF/15-30

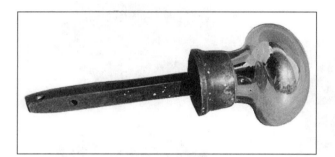

Mercury glass doorbell pull with brass shank and brass spindle, 1.75" dia., 4.5" long. HH/50-150

Entry-size cut glass mercury knob. SC/100-300

Set of mercury shutter knobs on pewter shanks. HH/50-150 all

Fancy mercury glass passage knob with a star-cut top. SC/100-300

Straight Shank Style

By the end of the century, most glass knobs were using a straight shank that was rolled around the knob tightly enough to keep it from slipping. The generic glass knobs of this style are of no interest to collectors, but the fancy pressed, cut and colored glass knobs are very desirable.

Large tapered, twisted rib knob with polished top and star center.

FF/30-100

Round, flat-top passage knob with Maltese cross interior. BC/15-30

Pressed glass oval passage knob with polished top.

HH/30-100

Round, flat-top passage knob with starburst interior and step-back brass shank.

BC/15-30

Carousel-shaped passage knob with some solarization. BC/15-30

A controlled bubble knob on a 20th century shank. FF/50-150

Multi-faceted "European" cut pressed-glass passage knob. XQ/30-100

A big, round glass ball, marked R&E, 1896. HH/30-100

A passage knob in the "Colonial" pattern by TEGO. FF/15-30

Cut & Faceted Glass

A very popular style of clear or colored glass doorknob was the faceted sphere. Some of these were hand cut and polished, while others were actually machine made. It often requires a close look to tell the difference. The best clue is to look for a seam or mold mark. Hand-cut crystal is usually distinctively heavy.

Entry-size knob, deeply cut and highly polished. XQ/50-150

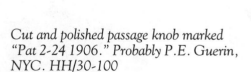

Cut and polished passage knob marked "Pat 2-24 1906." Probably P.E. Guerin, NYC. HH/30-100

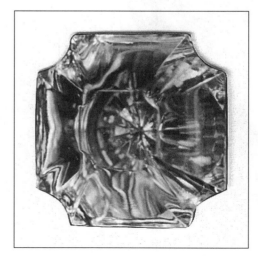

Square, notched-corner pressed-glass passage knob. HH/30-100

Faceted and polished passage knob with a nice sculpted waist.

HH/30-100

Pressed-glass passage knob with tapered sides and wheel-cut star design on top. BC/15-30

Magnum size hand-cut sphere with pointed top on a gilded rosette base and with a mirror star center. SC/100-300

Round hand-faceted passage knob.

FF/30-100

These knobs, plates, hinges and other items are some of our auction highlights over the past four years. All these pieces are of serious collector quality, especially when found in excellent condition and fine color.

A large reticulated plate (16" x 3") and passage knob cast in a floral pattern of daylilies. SC/300-500

Entrance knob in the pattern called the "Starfish." HH/100-300

Bronze door handle and thumb latch with a maple leaf thumb motif. Made by Welsh, c1930, 12" x 3.5". HH/100-300

Bronze entry knob in the form of a scallop shell. HH/100-300

Bronze entry knob with Wedgewood porcelain insert. These discs are found in both blue and green. The rosette is marked "Y&T." SC/100-300

Irish Setter entry knob by R&E, dated 1890 on the shank. Traces of gilding. SC/2000+

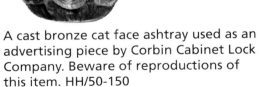

A cast bronze cat face ashtray used as an advertising piece by Corbin Cabinet Lock Company. Beware of reproductions of this item. HH/50-150

Bronze entry knob in the Treviso pattern by Yale, c1910. Marked on the shank. SC/300-500

Large sculpted door plate by R&E, c1870s. Note the rat bodies with eagle heads and the lion face surrounding the keyhole. SC/300-500

Silver-plated push plate by Corbin, c1874. Note the putti, birds and daylilies. SC/300-500

The "Motherhood" jumbo knob, marked "Russell & Erwin" on reverse. SC/2000+

Large Masonic door knocker/peep hole with lion head. SC/300-500

Heavy cast iron doggie doorknocker in old tan paint, American, mid-19th century. 6.5" x 4". SC/100-300

Pair of bronze neo-grec door pulls, c1870s. SC/1000+

Lion face passage knob and rose by H&D, c1870s, with neo-grec details. SC/1000+

An entry knob in the Napo pattern by R&E, c1890. Note the heavy relief with design influence from both medieval and Art Nouveau styling. XQ/50-150

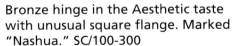

Bronze hinge in the Aesthetic taste with unusual square flange. Marked "Nashua." SC/100-300

A jumbo doorknob from Mallory Wheeler, c1870s, with a star design that reflects both the Union victory and the upcoming Centennial celebration. Note the strong Anglo-Japanese style of the rosette. SC/300-500

Bright red plastic passage knob with four-leaf clover. Marked "Made in USA." HH/30-100

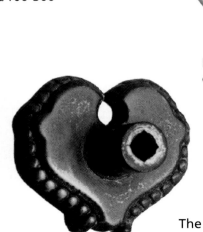

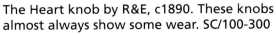

The Heart knob by R&E, c1890. These knobs almost always show some wear. SC/100-300

Pair of cut glass doorknobs in a variation on the hobnail pattern. SC/500+

The Judgment passage knob. Maker and story unknown. SC/500+

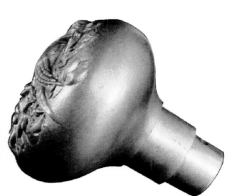

Entrance plate and knob in the Christensen pattern by R&E, c1899. SC/500+

Passage size "Flying Crane" doorknob, marked Russell & Erwin and part of its Japanese collection. SC/500+

A Jasperware passage knob with flowers and angels. HH/50-150

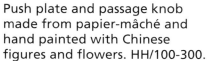

Push plate and passage knob made from papier-mâché and hand painted with Chinese figures and flowers. HH/100-300.

Bronze lion face, English, c1890. Pull the tongue and the bell rings. SC/1000+

Bronze passage knob with dragonfly. SC/500+

Entry knob from the Crow Wing Country Courthouse, Minnesota, c1900. SC/300-500

Triple scallop shell passage knob with pedestal shank and mushroom foot. SC/300-500

Door handle in the form of a smiling dragon. Recent age. HH/100-300

Bronze oval passage knob with standing lion. HH/50-150

Large worried-face lion face, probably by Schlag. HH/100-300

Bronze oval passage knob with standing lion. HH/50-150

Extra large door pull with Egyptian (Shriner/Masonic) motif. HH/300-500

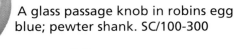

Several American hardware companies offered fired and decorated porcelain doorknobs before the Civil War. Plain white and black porcelain knobs were popular before the Civil War, but these, along with the generic brown/black mineral knobs, are of virtually no value to collectors today. However, a nice variety of decorated porcelain knobs was being produced at the same time and these are of considerable collector interest. Along with fancy porcelain, 19th century American hardware companies offered colored glass knobs. These most often are set in tapered shanks and are very collectable.

A glass passage knob in robins egg blue; pewter shank. SC/100-300

Porcelain passage knob with painted and fired decoration. Together with an early painted porcelain rosette and a painted porcelain keyhole cover. All from the 1860s. HH/100-300

A japanned porcelain passage knob from Nashua, c1879. Note the tapered brass shank. HH/30-100

A molded milk glass passage knob with acanthus leaf design; iron shank. HH/30-100

Porcelain passage knob with hand painted decoration in cobalt blue; pewter shank. HH/30-100

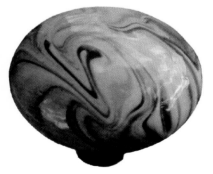

Tri-colored porcelain entry knob with blue and brown swirls. XQ/100-300

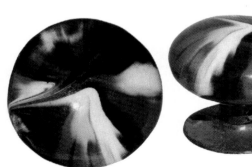

Multi-colored porcelain passage knob with iron shank and green painted iron rosette. SC/100-300

A knobby white porcelain passage knob with fitted rosette. HH/30-100

Entry size Dewdrop knob by Nashua, c1875. SC/100-300

Cobalt blue "Mushroom" knob on tapered shank, c1875. SC/100-300

Opalescent "Mushroom" knob on tapered shank, ca. 1880. HH/30-100

A petite black glass knob on an iron shank, possibly from the Ante Bellum. HH/30-100

Light blue milk glass passage knob with polished top and paneled sides. HH/50-150

Heavy, black glass octagon shaped entry knob with concave top and sculpted sides, c1870. XQ/100-300

Azure blue passage knob with star-cut top and paneled sides, c1900. HH/50-150

Passage knob with blue and brown glaze drizzled over white porcelain, set on pewter shank. HH/100-300

In 1874, Corbin created a line of enameled hardware and knobs, plates, locks and other pieces were offered in blue, black, red, green and white. It was an ambitious undertaking and the line was available for only a few years. Blue was apparently the most popular color, as it shows up the most frequently.

A cast iron passage knob with red, white, black and blue enamel. The rim is brass and the shank is dated 1884. Minor chips. HH/50-150

Blue enamel and gilded bronze entry knob by Corbin. SC/500+

A passage-size door plate in blue enamel and gilded bronze, 7" x 2.5". SC/300-500

This door handle and door plate were installed with a special-action mortise lock that also had an enameled front. SC/500+

A mortise lock with front plate inlaid with blue and black enamel. SC/50-150

An electric door bell lever from the 1880s, 5.5" x 2.5". SC/300-500

A strike plate with blue enamel, 6.25" x 1.25". SC/50-150

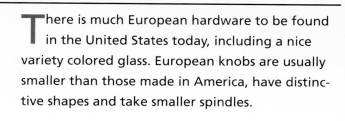

There is much European hardware to be found in the United States today, including a nice variety colored glass. European knobs are usually smaller than those made in America, have distinctive shapes and take smaller spindles.

Cased glass passage knob, white cut back to gold with knurled shank. SC/100-300

Cased glass passage knob, red cut back to silver with plain shank. SC/100-300

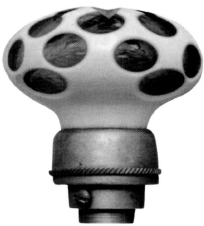

Cased glass passage knob, white cut back to green with knurled shank. SC/100-300

Authentic paperweight doorknob, c1850. Petite size, knurled shank and proper use of interior glass canes. SC/300-500

Millifiore doorknob from the 1950s (not 1860 as is written on the top), with stamped meal shank. FF/30-100

Unusual petite-size pressed glass knob set in well-made brass case and shank. HH/50-150

Round passage knob with 18th century courting scene. FF/50-150

Large ivory-colored porcelain knob on a fixed rosette, English, probably 20th century. HH/100-300

Passage knob with floral garlands painted in a quatrefoil design. HH/50-150

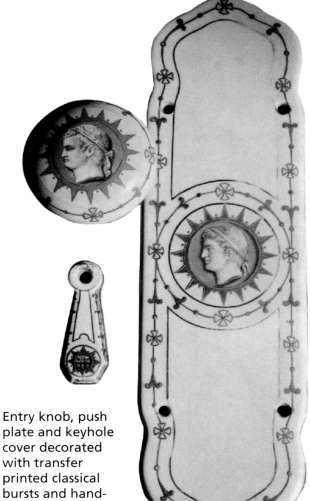

Small floral passage knob with raised slip decoration around a hand-painted bouquet. HH/50-150

Entry knob, push plate and keyhole cover decorated with transfer printed classical bursts and hand-applied gold borders. XQ/300-500

Oval passage knob with 18th century courting scene. FF/50-150

B y the turn of the century, production methods had improved to where a whole spectrum of colored glass knobs could be manufactured and marketed to compete with clear glass. These later knobs are set in the more contemporary "straight" shank and the glass often has a very manufactured look and feel.

Pressed glass passage knob in green, c1910. HH/50-150

Dark purple pressed glass passage knob, probably "cooked." FF/30-100

Smoky topaz pressed glass passage knob. HH/30-100

Amber colored entry knob with polished top. HH/50-150

Vaseline-colored entry knob with polished top. HH/50-150

Entry knob in robins egg blue with nickel shank. HH/50-150

Polished top pressed glass entry knob in cobalt blue. HH/50-150

The Aristocrats pattern from TECO features a star-cut top and gold-painted interior. BC/15-30

Naturally solarized, pressed glass entry knob with polished top. FF/15-30

Black and white sophistication: two deco knobs in black glass and two octagonal milk glass knobs. Minor scratches. BC/30-100

Cut glass knob in amber by P.E. Guerin, NY. XQ/50-150

Chapter 7

150 Years of Doorknob Designs

Doorknobs with Plates or Rosettes

It is a bonus to find a knob with the correct rosette or backplate, but more often these pieces have disappeared or have been mismatched. Every knob started life with a backplate or rosette. One of the enjoyable challenges of hardware collecting is finding the proper piece for a particular pattern.

Catalogs from the 1870s and 1880s often showed a particular doorknob escutcheon to be interchangeable with several different knob patterns. Most of the later Neo-Classical designs had specific plates for each, but many can still be mixed and matched successfully.

Condition of door plates and rosettes is important. Make sure it is not been bent or twisted, that the ferrule is not worn and the screw holes are not torn. Also, look at the reverse side for a maker's mark or an embossed name of the pattern. There are often foundry numbers embossed on the reverse as well, but these are generally not significant.

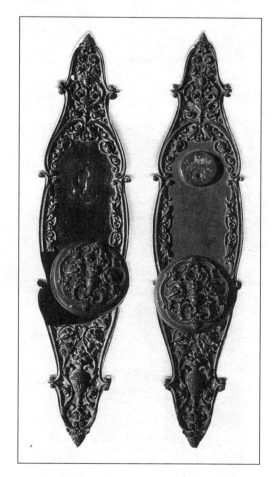

Pair of passage size knobs in the "Rice" pattern by Yale. Note the parasol form and the sunflower top. See the round top version in Chapter 2. FF/30-100

A pair of entry knobs and large backplates cast with urns and delicate flowers, c1890. SQ/100-300

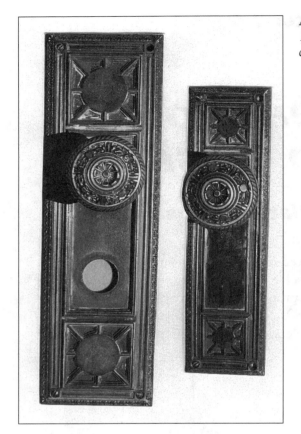

A pair of entry knobs and two plates (13" x 4" and 10" x 2.75") in the "Hadrian" pattern by Y&T, c1890. XQ/50-150

Large, heavily foliated door plate with Gothic-inspired melon-style knob; note the interesting tufted top. XQ/100-300

The Corinthian entry knob and plate (8.5" x 2") is an excellent example of 1890s style. XQ/30-100

194

A cast iron door plate and doorknob from the Statler Hotel in New York. Note the imperial eagle, the knight's helmet and the boar's head finial set above a crown. There is also a certain emphatic American symbolism with the logo lettering. XQ/100-300

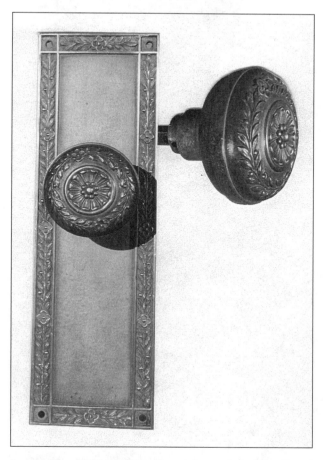

Large plate (10" x 3") with matching passage knob marked "YALE." BC/15-30

A group of passage knobs and hard to find small plates in the "Belforte" pattern by Reading, c1890. FF/100-300

Entry knob and double-keyhole backplate with strong
diaper pattern. XQ/30-100

Passage knob
with recessed,
banded edge and
scalloped rosette.
HH/30-100

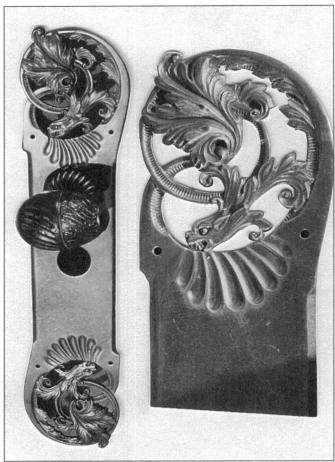

Jumbo-size plate with floral critters married up with a large
egg-shaped knob, 17" x 3.75". HH/50-150

Passage knob and plate in the "Mantua" pattern,
Reading Hardware, c1900. FF/15-30

Doorknobs with Locks and Other Pieces

Folks who wish to reuse vintage hardware are usually looking for "hardware sets" that include everything from the knob and rose, to the keyhole escutcheon and nightworks. Usually it is necessary to assemble various pieces of the same pattern, but often, one can find a large or even complete group at one time. These examples show the various pieces to look for.

Entry set by Norwalk, 1888. Large and small knob, large, double key-hole plate, rosette, fancy lock and nightworks. XQ/100-300

Passage set with high relief casting on the plate, two sunken center knobs and a decorative lock marked "PLCo."

HH/50-150

Entry set by A.G. Newman, c1890s: entry and passage knob, door plate 8.5" x 2.5", lock 8.25" x 4.25", strike 8.25" x 2.5", rose 2.25" dia., and keyhole escutcheon 3" x 1.5". HH/100-300

The "Portulaca" pattern by Penn Hardware, c1890. Note the little critters and the similarity to Reading's "Columbian" pattern. Entry and passage knobs, double-keyhole plate, 7.5" x 2.25", rose 2", and keyhole escutcheon 2" x 1". HH/100-300

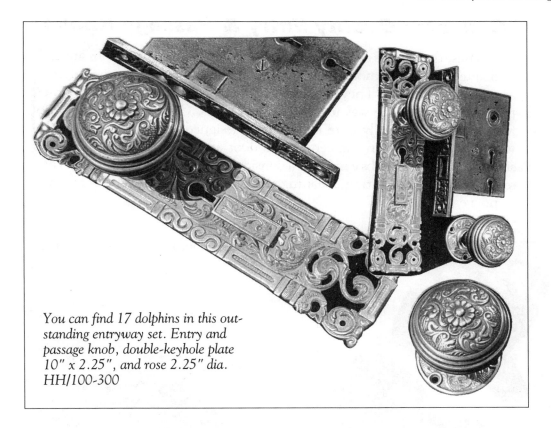

You can find 17 dolphins in this outstanding entryway set. Entry and passage knob, double-keyhole plate 10" x 2.25", and rose 2.25" dia. HH/100-300

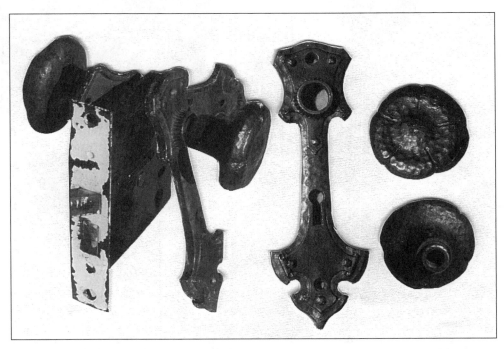

A pair cast iron Tudor-style passage knobs and backplates, 6.25" x 2", in a hammered finish, c1920, complete with mortise lock. BC/30-100

Collector Quality Entry & Passage Knobs

These doorknobs represent all styles and eras. Entry-size knobs are 2.5" in diameter. Passage knobs are 2.25". Smaller knobs in these same patterns are sometimes found. They were usually the doorbell pull, although sometimes the smaller size was used for screen doors. Oversize knobs are also found and these usually were individually designed. These "jumbo" knobs were more often set in the center of a door and used as a pull. Both the smaller and larger knobs can bring a considerable premium. Price ranges are for knobs in fine condition, meaning no damage, unpolished and with little or no wear.

The football knob, jumbo size and with a slotted shank. HH/30-100

Interesting flat-sided entry knob with daisy center. FF/30-100

"Crisscross" pattern, drum-form passage knob by Corbin, c1880. HH/30-100

Small, oval knob with wing designs and paneled top. HH/30-100

Passage knob marked "R&E, 1893," in a design that invokes the perfect splash. BC/15-30

The "Compass rose" entry knob, marked on back "Russell & Erwin Mfg. Co. New Britain Conn." HH/50-150

A passage knob in the "Olympus" pattern by R&E, c1905, featuring anthemions in high relief. BC/15-30

Passage size knob with foliate design in high relief. BC/15-30

Passage knob with heavily cast Greek anthemion, c1890s. BC/15-30

Passage knob with finely chiseled patterns on both obverse and reverse, c1885. HH/30-100

Passage knob by Norwalk with a strong Moorish design on top and a "Melon" pattern on the reverse, c1890. FF/15-30

Drum form passage knob with "basket weave" pattern on top and an unusual reeded shank. HH/30-100

An entry knob in the "Rocroy" pattern by Sargent, c1910.

HH/30-100

Passage knob with finely cast detail, c1880.

HH/30-100

Banded-edge passage knob by Lockwood, c1895, with a floral center, C-scrolls and fleur-de-lis. HH/30-100

Solid cast banded-edge passage knob with strong Neo-Grec designs. HH/30-100

Thick passage knob with swirled, sunken center motif and braided-edge design. FF/30-100

Interesting Gothic/Grec entry knob from Corbin, late-1870s.

FF/30-100

Cast bronze silver-plated entry knob with fine detailing and a well-tooled banded edge. HH/30-100

Entry knob with foliage inspired design from R&E, c1870, with banded edge. HH/30/100

Fine, small (2") Neo-Grec/Moorish knob with knurled edge, offered by Y&T in 1875 and Nashua in 1879. HH/30-100

Solid cast bronze jumbo-size center doorknob with original rosette. XQ/100-300

Neo-grec entry knob from Branford Lock Company. FF/30-100

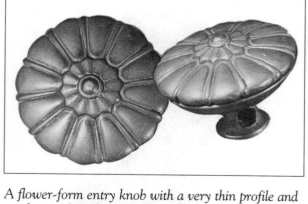

A flower-form entry knob with a very thin profile and mushroom footed shank. BC/30-100

Solid cast bronze passage knob with spiral form and button top, "Salem" pattern, marked "Y&T," c1910. XQ/30-100

Solid cast bronze passage knob, c1900, with strong Gothic antecedents. BC/15-30

Entry knob in the "Lorraine" pattern by Corbin, c1905. FF/30-100

An intricate pattern by Norwich, c1880: Greek palmettes, Aesthetic chevrons, Gothic quatrefoils and a checkerboard center.

FF/50-150

Lotus flower entry knob with a slotted shank. BC/30-100

205

Passage knob with an eight-pointed star within a ring of wreaths and flowers. HH/30-100

A set of Aesthetic-style knobs by Sargent, c1880. FF/50-150

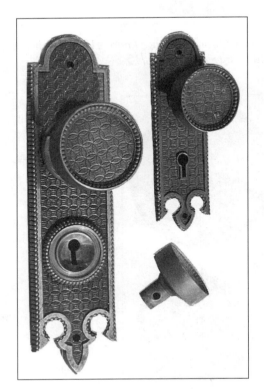

A striking diaper pattern is the highlight feature of these knobs and plates by F.C. Linde, c1890. XQ/50-150

A strong geometric pattern that originated with F. C. Linde, c1890 and was copied by other manufacturers, including Norwich. FF/30-100

Unusual Materials

American hardware has always taken the lead in experimenting with new materials. In the 19th century, there were doorknobs made from porcelain, clay, colored glass, wood, iron, gutta purcha and a variety of man-made composition materials. Later, America took the lead in using resin-based materials that evolved into what we now simply call plastic.

Gutta purcha was made from the sap of certain Asian trees and became a popular mid-19th century material that could be molded into very decorative forms. Many special material doorknobs are yet to be found and identified, so there is great potential here for energetic collectors. It is interesting to see how many pressed wood knobs have Neo-Grec motifs. This gives a good indication of their age.

Passage knob made from multi-colored clay: orange, brown, black and cream. HH/30-100

Passage knob made from speckled clay with an iron shank and iron rosette. HH/30-100

Passage knob made from fired mineral clay, with unusual brown/yellow salt glaze.

SC/50-150

Gutta purcha passage knob and rosette with all-over decoration. FF/30-100

Figural gutta purcha passage knob with a putto and dog running through the forest. Sculpted banded edge and reverse. HH/50-150

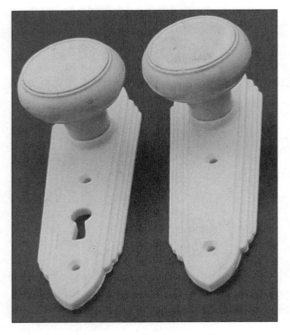

Pair of celluloid passage knobs and plates, c1930. BC/15-30

Clear acrylic octagonal passage knob with a blue rose interior, c1950. BC/30-100

Pair of clear and pink acrylic passage knobs with gold foil interior and chrome-plated shanks and rosettes, c1950. HH/30-100

Pressed wood passage knob with five-pointed star and sunflower center. HH/15-30

Pressed wood passage knob with butter center and Greek key border. HH/15-30

Pressed wood passage knob with flower top. HH/15-30

Pressed wood passage knob with Greek warrior head. HH/30-100

Pressed wood entry knob with Greek profile. SC/30-100

Pressed wood passage knob with sunflower top. HH/15-30

Pressed wood entry knob and wood and brass rosette with profile of Greek philosopher. HH/50-150

Chapter 8
Miscellaneous Builders' Hardware

Shutter & Sash Fittings

Homes in the 19th century invariably had an upper and a lower sash in each window opening that needed both lifts and locks. Also, many windows had interior shutters that required hinges, knobs and catches. All these fitting were cast with fine detail in many interesting designs and are very popular among collectors today.

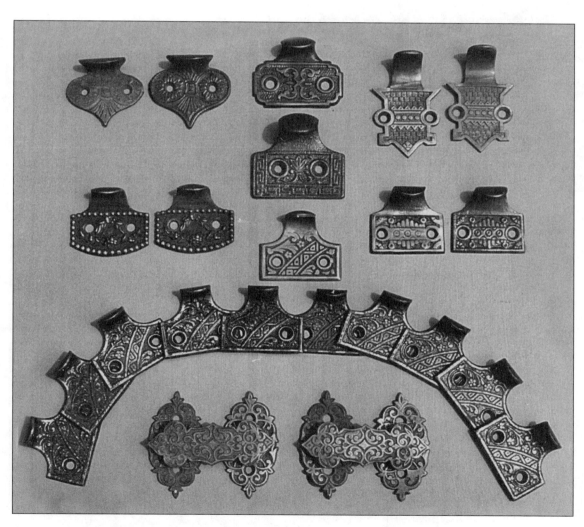

Group of tab-top sash lifts and a pair of fancy shutter latches. XQ/50-150 for 23 pieces

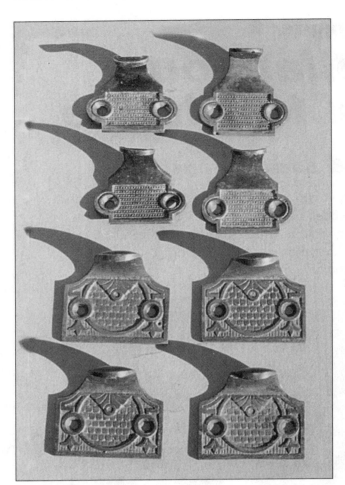

Group of eight bronze flush mount sash lifts, 1.75" x 1.75".

FF/30-100 for 8 pieces

Group of brass sash lifts, Pat. Oct 31, 1871, 2" x 1.75".

HH/30-100 for 10

Group of large sash lifts with incremental stops. Used in fancy railroad cars of the early 1880s. HH/30-100

Group of recessed window sash lifts. FF/30-100 for 10 pieces

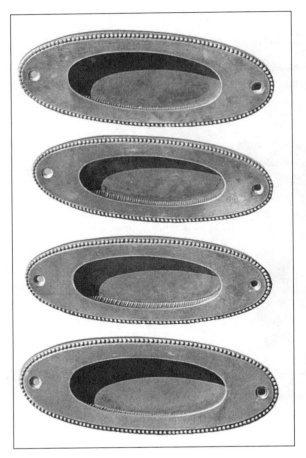

Set of four oval beaded, recessed sash lifts in Neo-Classical style, marked "YALE," 7" x 2.75".

HH/30-100

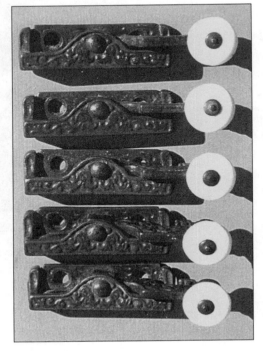

Set of cast iron sash locks with porcelain knobs, no keepers, 3.5" x 1".

HH/15-30 for 5 pieces

Group of bronze sash locks, all with keepers and porcelain knobs. HH/50-150

Group of three heavy brass sash locks, marked "Hopkins & Dickenson" and patented in '69, '73 and '75, 2.25" x 3". HH/30-100

Pair of high profile Neo-Grec sash locks with spring-loaded keepers, 3.25" x 3".

HH/30-100

Group of fancy silver-plated shutter knobs with fine detail and beaded shanks. SC/50-150

Selection of shutter latches from the 1870s. SC/50-150

Coat and Ceiling Hooks & Bin Pulls

Large homes required large-scale lighting and these chandeliers were often hung from fancy ceiling hooks. Likewise, electric ceiling fans needed hooks that were deeply embedded in the joists. Bin pulls are really a commercial furniture item, but they are found in so many interesting styles and designs that they have become an popular adjunct to door hardware collecting. Bin pulls were made mostly in cast iron, but sometimes in bronze. They are often marked and dated on the reverse. Beware of reproductions with iron ceiling hooks.

Group of bin pulls showing the wide variety of styles that can be found.

FF/50-150 for 12 pieces

Four bronze bin pulls with Aesthetic floral designs and castleated tops. HH/30-100

217

Group of brass sash lifts, "Pat Oct 31 1871."
HH/50-150

Two bin pulls, dated 1872, with female profiles.
HH/30-130

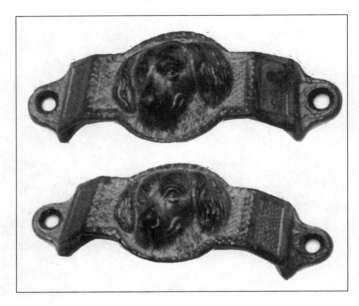

A pair of cast iron bin pulls with dog heads in old gold paint. HH/50-150

Pair of bin pulls with lyre decoration. BC/15-30

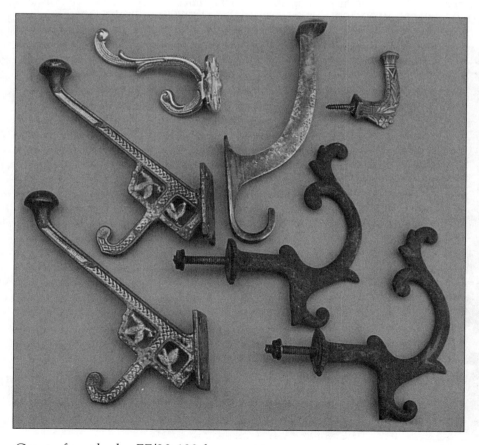

Group of coat hooks. FF/30-100 for seven pieces

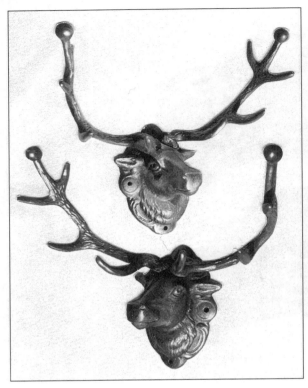

Pair of cast iron coat/hat hooks in the form of elk heads, c1890, 9" x 8". XQ/100-300

Set of three iron coat hooks with rusticated decoration, 3.75" long. BC/15-30

Group of figural brass hooks: dolphin, 4.5"; satyr head, 5.5"; two serpents, 6.25". HH/30-100

Heavily decorated chandelier hook, 3.75" long.

HH/15-30

Ceiling hook in the form of a dolphin, 3.75" long. HH/30-100

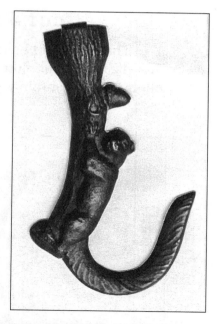

Ceiling hook in the form of a squirrel, 3.75" long. HH/50-150

Heavily decorated chandelier hook, 4" long.

HH/15-30

Ceiling hook in the form of a mermaid, 3.75" long. HH/50-150

Chandelier hook with Egyptian motifs, 3.5" x 2". HH/15-30

Boot Scrapes & Other Items

The breadth of hardware collecting extents to include all manner of miscellaneous items. Just a sampling is presented here. There are most certainly many great things yet to be discovered.

Nickel-plated cast iron center pull with Pharaoh head and winged scarab. HH/50-150

Cast iron boot scrape with an Irish Setter motif. HH/100-300

Group of cast iron French figural shutter locks. HH/50-150 for four pieces

222

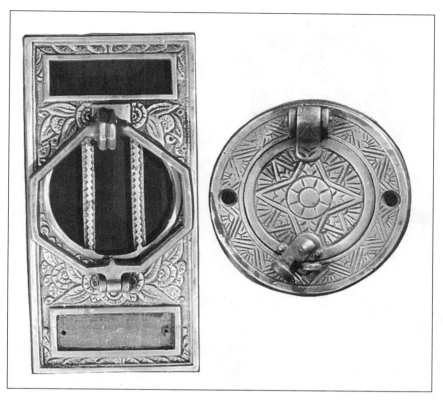

A Deco-style peep hole and door plate 6.5" x 3.25". HH/30-100

Bronze casement window latch in the form of a fist holding a rod, c1920, 3" across. HH/50-150

Bronze doorstop on marble base from…Union…12" x 15".

HH/50-150

Selection of small iron pieces: screen door handle, 5.25" long; pair of screen doorknobs, 1.25" dia.; unusual pair of small jamb latches with oak leaf decoration, 3.5" long. HH/30-100 for all

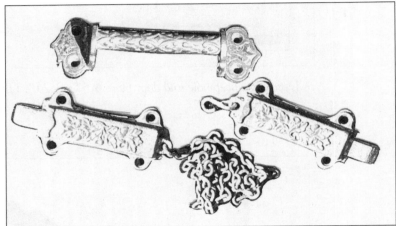

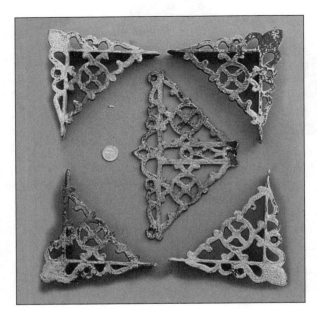

Set of iron screen door supports. FF/15-30

Hardware store counter display from Sargent, mounting board marked "L5N1762— 715JH." FF/15-30

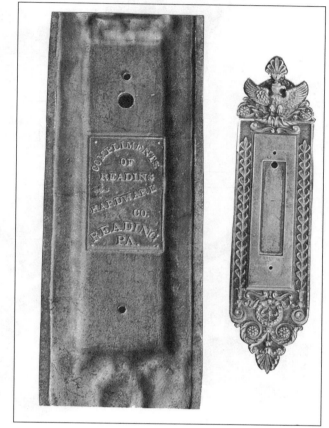

A thermometer holder with an eagle on the front and marked "Reading Hardware" on the reverse, 9.5" long. HH/50-150

A salesman sample window latch marked "IVES", 3" dia. FF/15-30

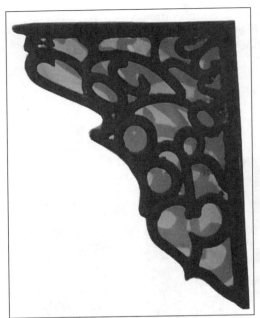

An iron bracket advertising with "Socks Bros." worked into the design, 12" x 9". HH/30-100

Bronze "GiltEdge" handle from Corbin Special Hardware, 7.25" long. HH/30-100

Two different "Security" knobs, 20th century. BC/15-30

Bronze plaque advertising Corbin lock boxes in the U.S. Postal Service, 4.75" x 6.5". HH/30-100

Chapter 9
They Loved the Lions

A Gallery of Feline Faces

The lion was probably the most popular animal motifs used by 19th century industrial artists. Here are a few good examples found in builders' hardware.

Entry door plate, 14" x 2.75", with exquisitely cast nautical details and lion head handle, 5", from a Newport mansion. SC/300-500

A cast iron bale handle with a lion face, probably English, 5.5" across. HH/50-150

Entry plate with a lion and two putti surrounding an oval cartouch, Corbin Special
Hardware, 18" x 4.25". HH/50-150

Two sets of mansion-quality French door handles with original rosettes. Marked "Y&T," c1900, 6" long and 3.5" from the door.
SC/1000+

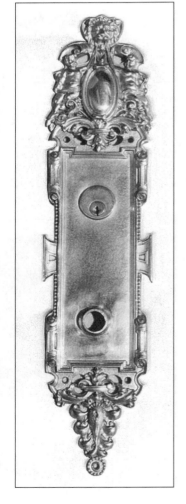

A bronze entry door plate with lion head above
two putti and a cartouch. This design is a modifi-
cation of another plate from Corbin Special Hardware, 16.5" x 3.75". SC/100-300

A lion head doorknocker, 5.5" x 3.75".
HH/30-100

Cast bronze lion doorbell. This item has been reproduced, 2.75" dia. SC/100-300

Oval entry knob with lion face and beaded border above and behind the flat paneled edge. SC/300-500

The Story of the Kreuzinger Lion

Ludwig Kreuzinger designed both the doggie and lion knobs and both received a patent on June 7, 1870. The reverse side of this example shows the MCCC/R&E mark, but many examples are found with just the R&E mark. These later example often show considerable wear, especially with the lettering, so look closely before paying a premium price.

The unmarked backplate, designed in the Neo-Grec taste, is not shown in any R&E catalog and may have been specially ordered. There is a Greek key at the bottom, braided laurel leaves around the doorknob and the dramatic akroter on top. Even though the keyhole cover is missing, this would be a major addition to any collection.

The Kreuzinger lion is a masterpiece of American industrial art, combining powerful scale, exquisite detailing and high drama. It represents the very best of American decorative hardware of the late 19th century. SC/2000+

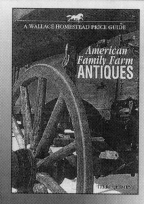

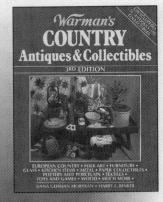

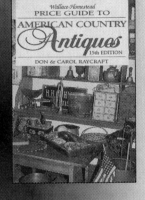
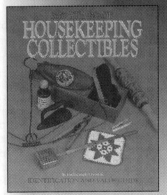